I would like to dedicate this book to pregnant women, that they may find the strength, love, and support to carry their children to term; to unborn children, who are the most vulnerable among us; to all children who need loving homes; to the adoptive parents who provide those homes; and to those who continue to peacefully fight for what they believe is right.

Acknowledgments

I would like to thank everyone who helped make this tremendous project possible. First of all, thank you to Jim Fletcher and New Leaf Press for approaching me with this incredible opportunity to share the history of the pro-life Democrats who fought and continue to fight for life.

I would also like to acknowledge and thank Congressman Jim Barcia for showing me that Democrats can be pro-life; Congressman Jim Oberstar for being the consistent voice and leader for pro-life Democrats in the U.S. Congress; Congressman Tim Roemer for his continued support for our efforts; Senator Ben Nelson for being a lone voice in the Senate; Congressman Chris Smith for his passion for protecting life and seeing beyond partisanship; Congressmen Tim Ryan, Bart Stupak, Lincoln Davis, and Congresswoman Marcy Kaptur for seeking middle ground to end abortion; and all the pro-life Democrats in Congress and around the country. I would also like to recognize Ambassador Ray Flynn for advocating for life beyond abortion.

My mentor and first vice president of DFLA, Bill Pierce, dedicated his life to promoting adoption as an alternative to abortion and bringing the Democratic Party back to Life. I continue this work in his memory.

The DFLA Board, both past and present, is an incredible group of the brightest minds and the biggest hearts, and they all truly believe in protecting life at all stages and also truly believe in the big tent of the Democratic Party. Their support on this project is greatly appreciated.

Thank you to Frank Sheridan, Janet Robert, Paul Contino, and Brian Keaney for taking the time to edit and re-edit. I also appreciate my friends Todd and Raquel Osborn for loaning me their laptop computer. It made things so much easier. Also, my friends Becka Allen, Michele Andersen, Angie Boone, Cristina Finch, Trey Mayfield, Sharon McKew, Tracy Melton, Jennifer Saunders, and Alice Wiesner for providing constant support for this project.

Most of all, I am grateful for my wonderful husband Chris; but for his patience, sacrifice, and support this book would not have been possible, and to my wonderful children, Jack and Kate, who are constant reminders of the beauty and sanctity of life.

Contents

Prologue

I have been asked many times how the Democratic Party could become entrenched as the party of abortion on demand, given their long history of fighting for the weak and vulnerable. They ask, "Isn't a baby in a mother's womb the best example of the most vulnerable in society?"

I have been asked more times than I can remember why I, someone that considers herself pro-life, remain in the Democratic Party when my party has pushed the abortion agenda for three decades. Conservatives encourage me to cast away my Democratic Party ideals and join the Republican Party, based entirely on one issue. By contrast, I am sometimes met with distrust from my friends on the Democratic side who think that I am not a real Democrat or a DINO (Democrat In Name Only).

These two questions led me to write this book. The history of the party is fascinating, particularly when we look at pro-life Democrats and why some left the party, why some stayed, and why some changed their position on abortion while others remained pro-life.

Few political debates are as heated and divisive as that of legalized abortion. This hot-topic issue is fraught with emotion on both sides of the divide. Pro-lifers are defending an innocent baby, who can do nothing to save him- or herself. Pro-choicers believe they are protecting the lives of women by keeping a medical procedure available for all women, even the poorest in the nation. These two vastly different positions have been adopted by each party, leaving very little middle ground for the average voter who believes that Republicans are pro-life and oppose abortion and Democrats are pro-choice and support abortion on demand.

Political parties listen to their constituencies, and the loudest voices form the party positions and platforms. Because the loudest voices set the agenda, sometimes the majority opinion is not represented. This is the case with the abortion issue. The Republican Party has embraced protecting the unborn and the Democrats have accepted the notion that abortion is a basic human right for women.

However, there is a growing realization that a majority of the population would like to see fewer abortions. In fact, a majority of Americans fall somewhere in between the rhetoric of the party platforms and don't fall clearly into either the pro-life or pro-choice categories. These simple terms can be used to describe less than half the population's views on a rather complex issue.

This great divide on abortion has been building for the last 30 years, and the biggest question is this: How did we get here? How did a party that fights for the underdog not lead the fight for the most innocent? Some say the party didn't even notice until 1992.

CHAPTER 1

Silencing the Troops

> "If we were truly the party of tolerance and inclusion as the conventions speakers claimed — just a great big circle of friends — what was the problem?" — Governor Bob Casey

Pro-life Democratic Governor Bob Casey of Pennsylvania was given the opportunity to speak at the Cooper Union School at a forum co-sponsored by the Village Voice on October 2, 1992. He was scheduled to give a speech titled "Can a Liberal Be Pro-life?"

The Cooper Union School had been founded by Peter Cooper, who grew up to be one of America's richest men. Never forgetting his roots and the barriers he faced in accessing education, he founded the Cooper Union School so immigrants and the working class could receive a proper education. The auditorium provided a place for discussions on political and social reform. Free lectures were provided on science, government, and important issues of the day. Presidents, including Grant, Cleveland, Taft, and Theodore

Roosevelt, had spoken in this historic place. Additionally, it was there that Abraham Lincoln delivered his famous anti-slavery speech, the "Right Makes Might" oratory, which opened the door for his presidency in 1860.[1]

When Casey walked up to the podium, pro-choice protesters attempted to silence him by shouting, "Murderers have no right to speak."[2] Nat Hentoff, who introduced Casey, urged the protesters to be silent and give the governor a chance to speak. The protesters continued their chant. Nat Hentoff then encouraged the governor to let him call the police to come and silence the protesters. Casey gallantly refused. He felt strongly about the importance of protecting the constitutional right to free speech.

After many unsuccessful attempts to silence the crowd, Casey conceded to the crowd. He said, "The Democratic Convention suspended the First Amendment and tonight you did the same thing," and stepped off the stage.

It was the Village Voice's first time sponsoring an event like this, and according to publisher David Schneiderman, it would be the last. He said of the event, "I had, in retrospect, this naïve faith that people would listen to another point of view."[3]

Historically, the Democratic Party has advanced the principles so eloquently spoken by Hubert Humphrey. *"The moral test of government is how it treats those who are in the dawn of life, the children; those who are in the twilight of life, the aged; and those who are in the shadows of life, the sick, the needy, and the handicapped."* The party has led the way to protect the weak and defenseless, to fight for civil rights and affordable health care, to provide a livable wage and safe communities, and to support the elderly and the disenfranchised. While every other class of underdog has enjoyed the advocacy and protection of the Democratic Party, the unborn children have been excluded. The Republican Party proudly took on the banner of protection for the unborn. Democrats abandoned the most defenseless of us all.

The Democratic Party didn't suddenly become the party that would fight for the right to abortion nor did all Democrats buy into the notion that we should fight for that right. Since the *Roe* v. *Wade* decision, various leaders, Democratic voters, and party activists have sent strong warnings that abortion should not be included in the party platform. They cautioned that the big tent must be open to those with opposing views or it would result in the eventual deterioration of the Democratic Party. The gradual transformation to advocate for abortion rights, which began shortly after *Roe*, reached its pinnacle at the 1992 Democratic Convention when Governor Bob Casey was silenced. While many Democrats had left the party during the Reagan years, pro-life Democrats left in droves after 1992.

A 1992 Gallup poll indicated that a majority of respondents (53 percent) believe that abortion should be legal in only certain circumstances. This trend has remained constant since the question was first asked in 1975. A 1992 CNN/ *USA Today*/Gallup poll found that only one-third of the respondents thought that abortion should always be legal.[4] That number dropped to 23 percent in a 1998 poll. Today, the number who believe that abortion should be legal in all circumstances is even lower.

In 1992, Democrats controlled of the House and Senate but felt frustrated by 12 years of Republican presidents.

The Democrats saw that they were losing ground and some strongly believed that abortion had polarized the party and should no longer be ignored. Surely, a respectful discussion of abortion led by a proven loyal Democratic governor would be allowed. It would display to pro-life Democrats across the nation that the party of the big tent welcomed those with differing views. The party needed to do something to reinvigorate itself, and Governor Casey was a strong enough leader and loyal enough Democrat to lead the effort to bring pro-life Democrats back into the party.

Governor Casey had just been re-elected as Pennsylvania's governor by more than a one million-vote margin, defeating a pro-choice Republican. He won 66 of 67 counties, a feat that has not been matched by any other statewide candidate.[5] While the media portrayed Governor Casey as a conservative Democrat, his record portrayed a more liberal progressive agenda. He had an impressive reputation of advocating and caring for the weak, the poor, and the disenfranchised. He stood for and advocated all the principles that the Democratic Party has historically championed.

His record in support of women included having appointed more women to his cabinet than any other Democratic governor and support for nutrition programs so low-income families would have access to nutritious meals.

After his initial attempts to pass universal health care in Pennsylvania, he proposed the Children's Health Care Act to establish the Children's Health Insurance Program (CHIP). CHIP provided uninsured children under the age of 12 guaranteed health care coverage and would expand by one every year to reach the goal of covering all children from 0 to 19.

Casey said of the bill, "This is no bare-bones program. It is a generous program. Any decent society should be generous to its sons and daughters."[6]

He advocated economic opportunity programs for women, children, and families and advocated programs to fight abuse of women, including funding domestic abuse and rape crisis programs. He championed women's rights and, in 1988, appointed the first black woman, Juanita Kidd Stout, to a State Supreme Court. Stout was a strong leader and advocate for success. She sought swift justice for gang members and received threatening letters during trials. She shared her outrage, not because of the threats, but because the letters contained many grammatical and spelling errors.[7]

As governor, Bob Casey rebuilt and reinvigorated the Democratic Party in Pennsylvania.

On the federal level, he raised money for the Democratic Party, including a key race where Democrat Harris Wofford defeated Republican Dick Thornburgh. Thornburgh, who served as the governor of Pennsylvania, also served as the Attorney General of the United States under Presidents Reagan and Bush. Paul Begala, who helped Casey win the governor's race in 1986, said of the race, "Save for Bob Casey, Harris Wofford would have lost. Casey rebuilt the party from ashes, and made it a better organization than the Republicans."[8]

Tragically, Senator John Heinz had died in a plane crash and the winner would serve out the remaining three years of his term. The heavy favorite in the November 5 special election was Thornburgh. Wofford's was a tremendous victory for Democrats, and Governor Casey played a crucial role in reclaiming the Democratic Senate seat. In any other situation he would have been considered a hero and would have been invited to speak at the 1992 Convention because of the victory reclaiming the Senate seat, his loyalty to the party, and his popularity in the fourth-largest state in the nation.

The theme of the 1992 Democratic Convention would be "unity and inclusion." Democrats had an incredible opportunity to stand up and lead on the most important civil rights issue of this decade. Democrats could finally have a dialogue within the party about abortion and lead the charge to protect an unprotected class. As they had led so many times before, this was their chance to change the direction the party was headed on abortion. However, "unity and inclusion" was not the message sent to pro-life Democrats, and instead the Democratic leadership sent a message that pro-life Democrats were not welcome in the big tent of the Democratic Party. They silenced their own troops, and took advantage of the distraction facing Republicans, who were not concerned about the Democratic Party in the 1992 presidential race.

Bush was ahead in the polls and more concerned about fighting off a challenge from third-party candidate Ross Perot. Republicans did not consider Democrats a viable threat because of their weakened status. This gave Democrats the opportunity to focus on their own issues without interference from the Bush campaign, which was worried about the growing popularity of Perot.

Although the party was weakened, the Clinton campaign generated electricity. Clinton showed a strong connection to the working people by focusing on his poor childhood and having been raised by a single mother. Clinton resonated with the American people. He spoke to key Democratic values including reforming health care, retraining the workforce, and working toward a better America. The party was moving toward the center, and Clinton was a new kind of Democrat. His "Putting People First Campaign" energized Democrats. Ironically, his more centrist platform called for cutting off welfare benefits after two years, the need for economic growth, support for the North American Free Trade Act (NAFTA), and allowing the states to enact death penalty statutes. It also included support for a "woman's right to choose."[9]

Pro-life Democrats learned at the 1992 Convention that they, too, could be in this new energized Democratic Party as long as they stayed silent. The party was looking to a bright, united future led by Clinton and Gore, and the party did not want or need dissenters.

The Clinton campaign was building strength and Clinton appeared to be uniting the party.

Pro-life Democrats were encouraged by the opportunity to reclaim the White House, but was the price too high? We supported the party that advocated for the working men and women of this country, the party that consistently fought for the underdog and all the injustices of the world. However, the party had a disconnect with the pro-life members of the party because they were advocating a woman's right to choose abortion for any reason at any time.

In 1992, pro-life Democrats learned that people who disagreed with the party would be ostracized even if they were loyal to the party. The pro-life position was a non-starter. So, many left the Democratic Party, unwillingly and regretfully. The party leaders did not realize they were alienating the very voters they would need to maintain control of the House 24 months later.

Governor Casey wanted the opportunity to represent and speak for those who believed that abortion was wrong at the 1992 Convention. In his book *Fighting For Life* he said, "I wasn't looking to stir up rancor. All I wanted was a chance to speak to offer a strong dissent based on the party's historic commitment to protecting the powerless."[10]

At a platform hearing in Cleveland, he requested the opportunity to speak at the Convention. He urged his fellow Democrats to identify those who agreed with the pro-life position and bring them back to the party. He was not asking for the party to change its position on abortion, only that the party consider a more centrist position.[11]

A Casey aide proposed that the platform include language to make abortion rare. The language stated, "Democrats do not support abortion on demand and believe that the number of abortions should be reduced." She, too, was cut off and treated with disrespect from other platform committee members. She needed 15 supporters to have a debate on the issue but only received 5 votes, so the issues were never even debated. Casey felt so passionately about speaking on behalf of pro-life Democrats that he continued his quest even after the defeat at the hearing.

Governor Casey wrote a letter to Democratic National Party Chairman Ron Brown, asking to represent the pro-life position at the convention. In his July 2, 1992, letter he wrote, "The Platform Committee draft has the effect of placing the national party even more squarely with the abortion-on-demand camp. I believe this is a serious mistake for the party and would like the opportunity to present this point of view, shared by many Democrats, to the convention." He thought this was a reasonable request. His request went unanswered.

He attended the convention and hand-delivered a letter to Texas Governor Anne Richards, chairperson of the convention. She, too, ignored his request. He finally received an answer in the form of a carbon copy of his letter, from the parliamentarian of the convention, saying his request was out of order and denied.

Yet Kathy Taylor, a pro-choice Republican woman who had worked to defeat Casey and supported his pro-choice Republican opponent, Barbara Hafer, was invited to speak along with five other pro-choice Republican women. The pro-choice Republicans were considered honored guests by the Democratic Party, while the popular governor from Pennsylvania was seated in the section farthest from the podium.

Taylor criticized President Bush's abortion record and said he had made an "unholy alliance with the most extreme anti-choice interest groups in America."

Taylor had worked to defeat Casey and supported his pro-choice Republican opponent, Barbara Hafer. Millions of Americans were able to hear her views about why abortion was empowering and a women's right to choose was essential. Adding insult to injury, a camera crew followed Taylor up to the Pennsylvania section to confront Casey about being out of touch with America on abortion. Casey, fortunately, was warned about the pending confrontation. He tactfully departed before the orchestrated and undignified confrontation could occur.

Many said that it was not Governor Casey's abortion stance that prevented him from speaking at the convention, but it was the fact that he did not endorse President Clinton. However, several speakers, including Governor Jerry Brown, spoke at the convention even though they had not yet endorsed Clinton. In fact, Brown supporters tried to silence the DNC chairman when he spoke the first night of the convention. They wanted their candidate to have a prime time speaking slot. The Brown delegates caused so much disruption on the convention floor that the chairman's remarks were barely audible. The state treasurer of California, Kathleen Brown, also had the opportunity to address the convention, even though she also did not endorse Clinton.

The 1992 convention highlighted women. Only one woman, Democratic Senator Barbara Mikulski, currently served in the U.S. Senate. Three others would join her that year — Senators Barbara Boxer, Dianne Feinstein, and Carol Moseley Braun, who at one time was pro-life.

In reality, it was the year of the pro-choice women. Kansas Governor Joan Finney was not included in the year of the women celebrations even though she was the first woman to defeat an incumbent governor in the United States. Dan Rather predicted her chances of winning were that of "a fortune cookie in an Italian restaurant." Elected in 1991 at the age of 65, she was the state's oldest governor and the state's first Catholic governor. She defeated a pro-choice Republican who outspent her by a margin of $2 million to $300,000. The National Organization of Women opposed her campaign because of her pro-life stance. She offered to second Al Gore's nomination but never heard a response.

Finney said of the convention, "They had women up there who had thought about running for office, or who had run, or who were in office. They had everybody up."

The party did find room for pro-choice Massachusetts State Rep. Barbara A. Hildt who was challenging seven-term pro-life Democrat Congressman Nicholas Mavroules in the Democratic primary. Congressman Mavroules did not attend the convention but was one of the cosigners of the Casey letter to the platform committee calling for moderation on the abortion issue.[12] After Representative Hildt defeated Congressman Mavroules in the primary, Republican Peter G. Torkildsen went on to win the seat that election year.

Leading pro-life Democrats, including Governor Casey, Sargent and Eunice Kennedy Shriver, and Nat Hentoff took out a full-page advertisement in the *New York Times* advocating the pro-life point of view. The "New American Compact: Caring About Women, Caring for the Unborn" called on all Americans to "adopt solutions that reflect the dignity and worth of every human being" and create policies "that are truly pro-women and pro-child." They further stated that the goal for dealing with crisis pregnancies was by "eliminating the crisis, not the child."

That same year, a model Democratic Convention was held in Portland, Oregon, for 12,000 students from the Pacific Northwest. High school students were assigned states and researched and represented their state. The convention had a strong presence from Democrats for Life who introduced two abortion planks. The platform contained the standard abortion rights language, but a minority plank was proposed to limit abortion to only rape, incest, and life of the mother.

A compromise nine-point proposal included incentives to reduce the need for abortion. Oregon State Representative Kevin Mannix told the assembly, "We must avoid the extreme positions" on abortion.[13] The student model Democratic Convention was years ahead of the Democratic Party in calling for moderation on the abortion issue.

The next election cycle, Democrats lost 54 seats, including 34 incumbents and, for the first time in 40 years, control of the House of Representatives.[14] The Democrats had held a 256-seat majority to the Republicans' 178 in 1992. The new Congress would begin with 230 Republicans and 204 Democrats. That same congressional session, Democratic Congressmen Nathan Deal, Greg Laughlin, Mike Parker, Jimmy Hayes, and Billy Tauzin changed parties.[15] All five were pro-life Democrats.

In 11 state legislatures, Republicans gained control of both chambers. Republicans have continued to gain, increasing the number from 6 in 1990 to 18 in 2000. In 2001, Republican state party platforms in all states but two contained planks that supported restrictions on abortion.

The parties weren't always so defined, but we have to look back at history to understand how the parties arrived at the positions they advocate today. It all started in Seneca Falls, New York.

Endnotes

1. See the history of The Cooper Union for the Advancement of Science and Art at http://www.cooper.edu/administration/about/Welcome.html.

2. "Protesters Silence Anti-Abortion Talk," *New York Times*, October 3, 1992, sect. 1, p. 28, Metropolitan Desk.

3. Ibid.

4. "Fluctuations, But No Major Change in Views on Abortion," *U.S. News*, January 20, 1998.

5. Interview with Pat Casey.

6. "Casey Signs Children's Health Insurance Bill," *The Intelligencer/The Record*, December 3, 1992, p. A-5.

7. Robert Thomas, "J.K. Stout, Pioneering Judge in Pennsylvania Is Dead at 79," *New York Times*, August 24, 1998.

8. Nat Hentoff, "Life of the Party, Nat Hentoff," *New Republic*, June 19, 2000.

9. William Jefferson Clinton, *Putting People First: How We Can All Change America* (New York: Times Books, 1992).

10. Robert P. Casey, *Fighting for Life* (Dallas, TX: Word Publishing, 1996).

11. *Valley Independent*, July 11, 1992.

12. Cathryn Donohoe, "Other Pro-life Democrats Got the Cold Shoulder at the DNC," *Washington Times,* August 31, 1992.

13. Advocates for Life Ministries, *Oregon Update*, July 1992, p. 11.

14. "Ten Years After the Republican Surge: 1994 and the Contract with America," presented at the 2005 State of the Parties Conference in Akron, OH, October 5–7, 2005.

15. "Switching Parties Through History," CBS News, May 23, 2001.

CHAPTER  2

The Beginning

"The history of mankind is a history of repeated injuries and usurpations on the part of man toward woman, having in direct object the establishment of an absolute tyranny over her." — The Declaration of Sentiments, 1848[1]

The Seneca Falls Convention and the Declaration of Sentiments forever changed the direction for women's rights. In 1848, women had limited rights. In most states, they were not allowed to vote, own property, or keep their own wages. Divorce and custody laws favored men, allowing the husbands to maintain control over the property and retain custody of the children. Professions such as medicine and law were closed to women because they were expected to become wives and mothers. Women from wealthy families were allowed an education, but it usually consisted of courses that would help them to become good homemakers.

As a very young girl, Elizabeth Cady Stanton overheard a conversation between her father, a judge, and an employee who was recently widowed. The widow had purchased a farm with her own money yet the property belonged to her late husband who willed it to their son, an irresponsible drunk. The law clearly stated that the property belonged to her husband and the will could not be overturned. In her innocence, Elizabeth thought if she ripped the pages out of the law book, it would make things right.[2] Later in her maturity she found the tools to achieve equality for women.

Prior to organizing for securing women's rights, Lucretia Mott traveled around the country, often without her husband, talking about the evils of slavery. She refused to use cotton and other "slavery-produced" goods. Mott attended the 1840 World Anti-Slavery Convention, but she and other women delegates were refused seats by the male organizers of the meetings. The women, including Susan B. Anthony, were seated in segregated quarters at the convention and left with a new goal. They vowed to fight for equality for women.

Not until eight years later would the women gather to fight for women's rights. In 1848, Elizabeth Cady Stanton drafted the Declaration of Sentiments, which was modeled after the Declaration of Rights.

The Declaration of Sentiments stated, "All men and women are created equal." It further called for women's rights to own property, to vote, and to enjoy an equal stance in society. Two hundred women and 40 men attended the conference on women's rights on July 19, 1848. Though seeking equal rights and equal responsibility for women, they followed the conventions of the times. Lucretia Mott's husband, James, chaired the meeting because it was not a woman's role to conduct political discourse.[3]

The women who wrote and signed the Declaration of Sentiments took great risks to gain equal treatment under the law. Opponents criticized the Declaration of Sentiments and chastised the women and men who supported the cause. The *Lowell Courier Editorial* read:

> "Progress" is the grand bubble which is now blown up to balloon bulk by the windy philosophers of the age. The women folks have just held a Convention up in New York State, and passed a sort of "bill of rights," affirming it their right to vote, to become teachers, legislators, lawyers, divines, and do all and sundries the "lords" may, and of right now do. They should have resolved at the same time, that it was obligatory also upon the "lords" aforesaid, to wash dishes, scour up, be put to the tub, handle the broom, darn stockings, patch breeches, scold the servants, dress in the latest fashion, wear trinkets, look beautiful, and be as fascinating as those blessed morsels of humanity whom God gave to preserve that rough animal man, in something like a reasonable civilization. "Progress!" Progress, forever![4]

Several co-signers of the Declaration withdrew their support because they were embarrassed by negative response from the public.

Women's rights conventions were held around the country to gain support. Elizabeth Cady Stanton, Susan B. Anthony, Lucy Stone, Sojourner Truth, and other pioneers for women's rights traveled the country defending the importance of all the components that made up the Declaration of Sentiments.

In 1854, they submitted 10,000 petitions to the New York legislature calling for suffrage and property rights for women. Elizabeth Cady Stanton addressed the New York legislature stating, "We ask no better laws than those you have made for yourselves. We need no other protection than that which your present laws secure to you."[5]

Eventually, gaining the right to vote became the central message of the group. That right would empower women by providing them with the opportunity to challenge and change other laws. It seemed logical that voting rights would be the means to achieve empowerment for women.

Abortion was not viewed as a woman's right in 1850. The consensus in society was that life began at conception, and the medical community advocated defining human life as beginning from conception. Eight years later, the American Medical Association opposed legislation that defined life as from the quickening.

The Civil War halted progress on women's rights, but women regrouped in 1867 when Stanton and Anthony launched a national campaign for women's rights. In 1868, they published the first issue of a weekly newspaper, *Revolution*, which advocated suffrage.[6] Their letterhead read, "Men, their rights, and nothing more; women, their rights, and nothing less."[7] The leaders of the fight for equality considered abortion evil and recognized that it was, in fact, harmful to women.

An 1869 version of the *Revolution* stated, "*No matter what the motive, love of ease, or a desire to save from suffering the unborn innocent, the woman is awfully guilty who commits* the deed. *It will burden her conscience in life, it will burden her soul in death; But oh thrice guilty is he who drives her to the desperation which impelled her to the crime.*"[8]

The women's rights movement celebrated its first major victory in 1878 when the first federal resolution to provide suffrage for women was introduced by California Senator Aaron Augustus Sargent. Thirty years had passed since the Seneca Falls Convention. The bill was stuck in committee for nine years and when it finally came before the Senate for a vote, it failed by a vote of 16 to 34.

In 1869, Wyoming became the first state to provide suffrage for women. Several states, including Washington, California, Kansas, Oregon, and Arizona followed. However, the federal legislation stalled in Congress.

The women continued to gain support by building coalitions of different groups. Susan B. Anthony and Stanton knew that the issue transcended party lines and stunned their Republican supporters by working with Democrats to add a plank to their platform in support of women's rights.

Women worldwide answered the call to action in support of equality for women when the International Women Suffrage Alliance formed and had their first meeting in 1902 with representatives from 11 countries. In 1946, they changed their name to the International Alliance for Women, and continue to fight for "equal rights, equal responsibility" worldwide. Today, they do not specifically mention abortion on their website. They advocate for the Convention on the Elimination of All Forms of Discrimination against Women (CEDAW), which has been ratified by 179 countries. The treaty is an international bill of rights for women. The agreement has not been approved by the United States because it advocates for reproductive rights — which assumes access to abortion.

At home, women were advocating for suffrage in both political parties and achieved their first victory in 1916. Both parties included language in their prospective platforms to extend the right to vote to women. The Democrats encouraged states to expand suffrage while the Republicans favored suffrage, but thought the individual states should decide.

Democrat Platform	Republican Platform
We recommend the extension of the franchise to the women of the country by the States upon the same terms as to men.	The Republican party, reaffirming its faith in government of the people, by the people, for the people, as a measure of justice to one-half the adult people of this country, favors the extension of the suffrage to women, but recognizes the right of each state to settle this question for itself.

President Woodrow Wilson initially opposed suffrage until the state of New York adopted a women's suffrage resolution.[9] He changed his position, but not until after Alice Paul led the "Silent Sentinels" in a protest in front of the White

House. The Sentinels were arrested and Paul subsequently went on a hunger strike to protest their accommodations. Congress finally took up House Joint Resolution 1 and passed it in the House on May 21, 1919. The Senate passed the bill two weeks later.

Tennessee ratified the 19th Amendment on August 26, 1920, and finally women achieved the right to vote. Seventy-two years had passed since the Seneca Falls Convention.

Elizabeth Cady Stanton, Susan B. Anthony, and Lucretia Mott achieved their goal; however, they did not live to exercise their franchise. Most women were satisfied with this great victory and thought they were done. They believed that the right to vote would mean automatic equality for women and that there was no need to fight further.

Others saw suffrage as only a beginning, but no one was entirely sure where women should go next. The right to vote was a tangible prize. After that was achieved, there wasn't another obvious tangible goal. Alice Paul wrote and proposed an Equal Rights Amendment to the Constitution in 1923. The idea fizzled because a majority of the women believed they had already won the war. It would be decades before women began to rise to positions of influence and have the ability to challenge unjust laws and perceptions about women in the workforce.

Movements are characterized by different leaders who step up to promote the ideas that they believe will advance their cause. Personal agendas, not necessarily the best ideas or the strongest leaders of the movement, advance the ideas taken by the group. To make incremental changes in any movement, a thorough spirited discussion and debate is essential. The feminist movement needed to unite behind a new leader, new idea, and a new debate if they were going to continue to work toward equal rights.

Margaret Sanger, knee-deep in the trenches, emerged as the new leader. She is a confusing and controversial character who advocated for birth control, population control, and eugenics.[10] She was largely influenced by socialists and advocates for free love that she met at the Ferrer School. She was also influenced by years of living in "tamed domesticity" as a wife and mother, her mother's early death, and the low-income women she met as a nurse.

She closely followed the work of Madeleine Pelletier who made the case in France in 1913 that women and only women should decide on whether or not to carry a child to term. Pelletier was an advocate for population control through birth control or abortion. In fact, Pelletier performed abortions and claimed that they would be a lot safer if they were legal.

Sanger believed that women deserved the right to control their own bodies, the right to choose when to start families, and the right to the sexual freedom that men enjoyed. The combination of these three would mean power and thus equality. Sanger herself had her share of sexual liaisons outside of marriage.

Her early writings earn sympathy for the plight of the women who were continuously pregnant and did not have the money or resources to care for additional children. However, her later embrace of eugenics and her position that birth control was a means to an end to create the perfect race tainted the good she claimed to be doing in the beginning.

Sanger, a nurse who worked with low-income pregnant women, struggled with the effects of a non-existent health care system. She witnessed preventable deaths from pregnancy and also the wounds inflicted on women attempting abortion at home. She saw women with 9, 10, or 11 children begging for her help to prevent another pregnancy. Because her mother died of tuberculosis at age 49, Sanger blamed the toll ten pregnancies had taken on her mother's body. Poverty also contributed to her mother's downfall, and Margaret vowed not to be poor. She married twice, to wealth.[11]

Sanger's thinking arose from her mission to help women control their childbearing decisions. Maternal mortality rates were high because most women delivered at home with the assistance of a midwife. According to the most recent Center for Disease Control report on Pregnancy-Related Mortality Surveillance, 850 women per 100,000 (0.85 percent) died as result of pregnancy in 1900. By 1982, the number had dropped to 7.5 women per 100,000 (0.01 percent).[12] The decline can be attributed to the introduction of penicillin and that more women started delivering in hospitals with the assistance of doctors.

The women Sanger met were desperate to prevent future pregnancies but did not know how to and had few options. Women, by convention and law, could not refuse relations with their husbands and were often blamed for resulting pregnancies. Men could not be convicted of raping their wives until 1976 when Nebraska became the first state to allow a wife to file charges against her husband for rape.

In July of 1921, Sanger was called to help save Sadie Sachs, a poor 28-year-old woman who attempted to abort her fourth child. Illegal abortion, whether self-induced or performed by a doctor, was heavily discouraged for moral reasons. The 1921 Lippincott's nursing manual warned nurses not to associate with doctors who performed abortion, "for you could not afford to associate in private nursing with a criminal or malefactor of this type."[13] She was desperate not to have another child because her family did not have enough money to provide for their three existing children. The woman succeeded in aborting her fourth child and survived, but knew that she would not survive another. She pleaded with Sanger to share the secret of preventing pregnancy. Sanger ignored the pleas from the desperate woman and told her she would check back in a few weeks. The attending physician told the women the solution was easy — "Tell Jake to sleep on the roof." He further stated that "she can't have her cake and eat it, too."

Three months later, Sachs died from another attempted abortion. The story may have been apocryphal, but Sanger took it seriously and it influenced her work.

Sanger realized that the right to vote had not fulfilled its promise of full equality for women, but Sanger believed she knew what would. Sanger took the reigns of the feminist movement with a new mission and message. She wrote, "I was resolved to seek out the root of evil, to do something to change the destiny of mothers whose miseries were as vast as the sky." Her later writings revealed much more about the misery she was referring to as she veered dangerously into eugenics.

In a November 1921 edition of the *Birth Control Review*, she wrote, "More children from the fit, less from the unfit

— this is the chief issue of birth control." The same edition claimed that the goal of birth control was "to create a race of thoroughbreds." In 1939, she wrote, "We do not want word to get out that we want to exterminate the Negro population."[14] In an August 15, 1926, speech before the Institute of Euthenics at Vassar College, she talked about the billions of dollars spent "for the care and maintenance and perpetuation of those undesirables." Further stating that the "American public is taxed, heavily taxed, to maintain and increase a race of morons."

In her fight for the right to contraception, she decided that the legislative process was too slow and the only way to advance her goals was through the judicial process. She published the *Women Rebel*, a magazine for working women, in 1914, but the post office refused to mail it, citing a violation of the Comstock Law prohibiting the publishing of obscene material. She was indicted on nine counts by the Department of Justice and faced the possibility of one year in jail. She fled the country to avoid the trial, leaving her children in the care of others. Sanger eventually returned and was convicted of distributing obscene material. However, she was victorious because the trial changed public opinion about birth control.

On October 16, 1916, she opened a clinic to distribute information on contraception and was once again arrested. She told her clients, "Abortion was the wrong way — no matter how early it was performed it was taking a life; that contraception was the better way, the safer way — it took a little time, a little trouble, but was well worthwhile in the long run, because life had not yet begun. . . ."[15] In a meeting with a Russian doctor, she emphasized that contraception rather than abortion was a better way to handle family planning. Of the Russian abortion issue, she said, "Four hundred thousand abortions a year indicate women do not want to have so many children; in my opinion it is a cruel method of dealing with the problem because abortion, no matter how well done, is a terrific nervous strain and an exhausting physical hardship."

The 1920s brought about new ideas, and the expansion of capitalism resulted in a prosperous America. The daughters of the women's rights movements were uninterested in politics and embraced the Roaring Twenties of fun and independence. Women made advancements in sports, education, and employment. The National American Women's Suffrage Association changed its name to the League of Women Voters and started training women on issues and campaigns. The National Women's Party turned their attention to passing the Equal Rights Amendment and ending legal discrimination against women.

Women were making gains. Families had jobs and money. Women had the right to vote. However, motherhood and domesticity were the primary career choices for women. Even women who attended college were forced to take courses on marriage and family.

In 1921, Sanger founded the American Birth Control League to help women prevent pregnancy. She believed that women could not exercise their right to better jobs, a proper education, or achieve full equality if they were home with children or continuously pregnant.

Planned Parenthood credits Margaret Sanger for establishing "a woman's right to control her body" as "the foundation of her human rights" and thus equality with her male counterpart.[16]

Sanger, leading this "second wave" of the feminist movement made the right to choose the main tenet for achieving full empowerment for women. Sanger saw the negative aspects of pregnancy and family and said, "I knew something must be done to rescue those women who were voiceless; someone had to express with white hot intensity the conviction that they must be empowered to decide for themselves when they should fulfill the supreme function of motherhood." Little thought was given to the unborn child.

While perhaps she thought abortion was the taking of a life, she laid the groundwork for the argument used today that equates the "right to choose" with the right to abortion. The second wave argued that no man should have a say over what women do with their own bodies and that women should have the same sexual freedom (without responsibility) that men do.

The fight centered on what was right for the individual rather than what was morally or ethically right. There was no price too high to pay to advance one's personal rights. In 1926, author Winifred Holtby wrote about the new feminist movement that had emerged following several years of inaction. She stated, "The New Feminism emphasizes the importance of the 'women's point of view,' the Old Feminism believes in the primary importance of the human being."[17]

The "old feminists" did not accept that abortion was necessary to advancing women's rights. Elizabeth Cady Stanton said, "When you consider women have been treated as property, it is degrading to women that we should treat our children as property to be disposed of as we see fit." Susan B. Anthony also had strong pro-life views and called abortion child murder. Alice Paul wrote, "Abortion is the ultimate exploitation of women."

The Great Depression halted the advancement of women's rights because the stock market crash caused desperation for food and work. Franklin Delano Roosevelt's New Deal revived the women's movement and changed the government's responsibility to include support for single mothers, the poor, the elderly, and the unemployed, and made social welfare a responsibility. The New Deal brought promises of advances for women and blacks. Former actress and Congresswoman Helen Gahagan Douglas (D-GA) championed the New Deal policies and was an ardent supporter of equal rights. Elected in a minority district, she was the first white representative to hire black staff and appoint black students to military academies. In 1945, Douglas introduced legislation to provide equal pay for equal work, which didn't pass Congress until 1961. Republican Richard Nixon challenged and defeated Congresswoman Douglas in a dirty campaign where he accused her of being pink (Communist) right down to her underwear. She dubbed him "Tricky Dicky" as a result of the campaign tactics.

World War II empowered women as they entered the workforce in great numbers because the men went off to war. Rosie the Riveter posters showed a strong woman and enticed women to enter the workforce. Kay Kyser wrote a song about the women riveters called "That little frail can do/more than a male can do."

Unborn children started to gain legal rights in 1946. In *Bonbrest* v. *Kotz*, the court ruled that there were three victims in the case of a baby injured during delivery. The mother, the father, and the baby all were awarded compensation for the injury.

Women felt empowered, but the Equal Rights Amendment stood still for now and a majority of men and women still thought that a women's place was in the home. And, there was a new war brewing — one over civil rights.

Endnotes

1. *The Declaration of Sentiments*, Seneca Falls, New York, 1848.

2. Sara M. Evans, *Born for Liberty: A History of Women in America* (New York: The Free Press, a division of Simon & Schuster, Inc., 1991).

3. Ibid., p. 95.

4. Editorial on Seneca Falls Convention from the *Lowell Courier*, 1848.

5. Christina Hoff Sommers, *Who Stole Feminism?* (New York: Simon & Schuster, 1994).

6. Suffrage is the civil right to vote or the exercise of that right. In that context, it is also called political franchise or simply "the franchise."

7. http://www.susanbanthonyhouse.org/

8. "America's Earliest Feminists Opposed Abortion: Pioneering Activists Such as Susan B. Anthony and Alice Paul, Says the Writer, Called Abortion 'The Ultimate Exploitation of Women,' " *Chicago Sun Times*, January 8, 2006, p. B3.

9. U.S. National Archives & Records Administration, The Constitution: The 19th Amendment.

10. Eugenics is a social philosophy which advocates the improvement of human hereditary traits through social intervention. The goals have variously been to create more intelligent people, save society resources, lessen human suffering, and reduce health problems. Proposed means of achieving these goals

most commonly include birth control, selective breeding, and genetic engineering.

11. Mark Herring, *The Pro-life/Pro-choice Debate* (Westport, CT: Greenwood Press, 2003).

12. Center for Disease Control, Pregnancy-Related Mortality Surveillance — United States — 1990–1999.

13. Jimmy Carter, *An Hour Before Daylight* (New York: Simon and Schuster, 2001).

14. "Unnatural Selection, Planned Parenthood Campaign Against Minorities," *Diversity* (March/April 1992).

15. Jill Kerr Conway, *Written by Herself* (New York: Vintage Books, 1992).

16. Planned Parenthood website (http://www.plannedparenthood. org/pp2/portal/files/portal/medicalinfo/birthcontrol/bio-margaret-sanger.xml).

17. Paul Berry and Alan Bishop, editors, *Testament of a Generation: The Journalism of Vera Brittain & Winifred Holtby* (London: Virago, 1985).

CHAPTER 3

Honest and Open Debate and a New Leader

"From the time of Thomas Jefferson, the time of that immortal American doctrine of individual rights, under just and fairly administered laws, the Democratic Party has tried hard to secure expanding freedoms for all citizens. Oh, yes, I know, other political parties may have talked more about civil rights, but the Democratic Party has securely done more for civil rights." — Hubert Humphrey[1]

In 1948, African Americans were an unprotected class. Laws segregated schools, buses, and restaurants. The poll tax in 11 states made it difficult for poor black families to vote. Miscegenation laws prohibited interracial marriage. Shops and restaurants had "whites only" signs hung on their doors and there were separate drinking fountains for blacks and whites.

The Civil Rights movement was just beginning. The historic ruling *Brown* v. *the Board of Education*, which desegregated our schools, was still seven years off. Rosa Parks was yet still sitting in the back of the bus. Ten years would pass before the governor of Arkansas used the National Guard to prevent nine black students from attending a public high school in 1957.

The Civil Rights movement was just beginning and President Harry Truman, who was running for re-election, was at the center of the battle. Many were doubtful of his ability to win against Republican Thomas E. Dewey. The top political reporters all agreed that Dewey would not only win, but would serve for eight years. Both parties attempted to recruit General Eisenhower, but he declined. The Republican Party had just won control of the House and Senate in 1946.

There was a question about whether the Democratic Party would continue to be one party or break into two because of the conflict between the northern and southern states. The northern block wanted to push for civil rights and equality, while the southern block valued state's rights to maintain the status quo. James Loeb, director of Americans of Democratic Action thought if the Democratic Party was "going to go down," they would go down fighting for something.[2]

The time for civil rights had come.

Truman supported civil rights, and issued an executive order on December 5, 1946, to establish a Commission on Civil Rights. He wanted a report on the current status of civil rights in the United States. On June 29, 1947, he addressed the NAACP in support of equal rights for blacks stating, "As Americans, we believe that every man should be free to live his life as he wishes."[3] In October, the commission report explained the need for a legislative resolution to secure the rights for minorities. They recommended several initiatives, including urging the president to establish a permanent commission on civil rights, enact federal protection against lynching, and grant citizenship to minorities. In Truman's message to Congress on February 2, 1948, he urged Congress to enact the recommendations and end segregation and discrimination. However, to maintain peace in the party, he instructed party leaders to keep his "civil rights" package out of the 1948 platform and encouraged the drafters to use the weaker 1944 compromise language that said,

> We believe that racial and religious minorities have the right to live, develop, and vote equally with all citizens and share the rights that are guaranteed by our Constitution. Congress should exert its full constitutional powers to protect those rights.

The plan, he thought, would appease both the northern and southern delegations by neither advocating for nor against extending civil rights to blacks and keep the party together. Few in the party wanted to rock the boat on the platform because Truman's chances of winning were slim and they did not want to risk losing any votes.

Party leaders underestimated the determination of the 37-year-old mayor of Minneapolis, Hubert Humphrey. Humphrey had lost his first mayoral race in 1943, but was elected in 1945. In 1948, he was not only a delegate to the Democratic Convention, he was also a Senate candidate. Minnesota had never elected a Democratic senator.[4]

"Humphrey and some of the kids," as party leaders and the media referred to them, believed that the platform should contain strong civil rights language. In fact, the kids' headquarters was at a fraternity house at the University of Pennsylvania. Humphrey, Andrew Beimiller, and Joe Rauh on behalf of the Americans for Democratic Action, decided to proceed with plans to amend the platform.

The fight behind closed doors was fierce and tempers were hot — and so were the temperatures. There was no air conditioning and the summer heat was sweltering. Democratic Leader of the Senate Scott Lucas called Humphrey a pipsqueak during the debate. The oldtimers saw Humphrey's plan as a threat that would give the election to the Republicans and split the Democratic Party into two. Their efforts failed by a vote of 70 to 30, with Convention Chairman Sam Rayburn, Chairman of the Platform Committee, Senator Francis Myers, and Democratic Party Chairman McGrath all opposing Humphrey.

Traditionally, Convention procedure dictated that if you lost in the platform committee, the fight was over. The platform meetings were behind closed doors and private. If the fight were brought to the floor, it would be open to the media and to the American public. There was no television yet, but the Convention was broadcast on the radio.

Humphrey considered going to the floor with a minority report on civil rights. Minority reports can play a crucial role in moving a party in a new direction. The platform committee prepares a platform for the party by building a coalition of support around the issues they feel best represents the party views. They hear testimony and discuss the issues they should put in the platform. This process is done every four years, and the presidential candidate has sway over what the platform states. Minority reports are generated when ideas come before the committee and fail. However, if a certain percentage of representatives on the platform committee support the proposed amendment to the platform, the minority report can be brought up for a vote at the convention.

It was a hard decision for Humphrey. Many said it would ruin his political future if he continued with this effort. Some senators did hold it against him when he served in the U.S. Senate. Even his own father, who was the chairman of the South Dakota delegation, expressed concern, but ultimately supported his son. In a private meeting in Humphrey's fourth floor hotel room at the Bellevue Stratford, the senior Humphrey said, "This may tear the party apart," but "you can't run away from your conscience."

The minority report at the 1948 Convention called for the party to consider adding a civil rights plank in the Democratic platform. Just before his speech, a nervous Humphrey turned to Ed Flynn and asked for his opinion on the minority report. Flynn responded, "You're damned right. You go ahead, young man. We should have done this a long time ago." Flynn pledged to talk to other party leaders including Jake Avery from Illinois and mayor of Pittsburgh David Lawrence. Both approached Humphrey and said they would back him. In his speech, Humphrey addressed the crowd who thought he was infringing on states' rights, "The time has arrived for the Democratic Party to get out of the shadow of states' rights and walk forthrightly into the bright sunshine of human rights."

A furious debate ensued prompting the Alabama and Mississippi delegations to walk out of the convention waving the Confederate flag. The Civil Rights Amendment was approved by 69 votes 651½ to 582½.[5] The platform stated:

> The democratic party [sic] is responsible for the great civil rights gains made in recent years in eliminating unfair and illegal discrimination based on race, creed or color. The Democratic Party commits itself to continuing its efforts to eradicate all racial, religious and economic discrimination. We again state our belief that racial and religious minorities must have the right to live, the right to work, the right to vote and full and equal protection of the laws, on a basis of equality with all citizens as guaranteed by the constitution.[6]

The young guard had beaten the old guard on the plank. "The kids" carried Humphrey all the way back to the fraternity house for celebration. Senator Strom Thurmond led 35 delegates out to form the Dixiecrat Party which earned 38 electoral votes in the 1948 election.

Silencing the troops is ultimately destructive because good things can come out of a healthy debate. Despite the disagreement, strong debate, and belief that this kind of discussion would kill the Democratic Party, President Truman defeated Dewey in 1948 and Democrats won 75 House seats to take back the majority. The Democrats had previously held 188 of the 435 seats. The election gave them a 263 majority. The Democratic Party not only survived the civil rights debate, it was a stronger party for having allowed voices to be heard and statements to be made.

Only one million people had television sets, so the convention remained a private affair. Today, the political convention equates to large orchestrated productions because there is gavel-to-gavel coverage by many different television stations. The parties don't want to broadcast their differences.

The Democratic Party had led the charge on the greatest civil rights issue of that era. We had a disconnect with the American people, but we, as a party, were willing to fight for injustices in America even if it meant dividing our party. It was a contentious debate, but one that ultimately made our party stronger. The willingness to debate in an open forum and let people talk about the important issues of the day was something that was allowed in 1948. Still, acceptance of civil rights among the majority of Americans did not occur until the 1960s Civil Rights movement when television opened the eyes of the public to the injustices. Similarly, the advent of the ultrasound machine has changed the opinion of many on when life begins.

Endnotes

1. 1948 Democratic National Convention Address.
2. Truman Presidential Museum and Library, Oral History Interview with James I. Loeb, June 26, 1970.
3. Harry Truman, *Memoirs of Hope* (Garden City, NY: Doubleday & Company, Inc., 1956).
4. Hubert Humphrey, *Beyond Civil Rights* (New York: Random House, 1968).
5. "The Line Squall," *Time*, July 26, 1948.
6. *Lincoln Journal*, July 15, 1948.

CHAPTER 4

The Right to Privacy

> "The problem that has no name — which is simply the fact that American women are kept from growing to their full human capacities — is taking a far greater toll on the physical and mental health of our country than any known disease." — Betty Friedan[1]

In the 1950s, women were pulled back into traditional roles after the men returned from the war. A majority of the women wanted to continue to work but were forced home. The skilled jobs they held during the war were closed to them and the only jobs available paid half of their wartime salaries.

Both political parties diminished the role of their women's divisions. The Democratic Party integrated the women's division into the committee operations. However, it had the effect of stripping their budget and usurped their power and decision-making authority. India Edwards, who served as Director of the Women's Division, was a trusted advisor to President Truman, and believed that it was a deliberate act by Chairman Steve Mitchell.

She recalls that the chairman "outsmarted her." India thought, and rightfully so, that Mitchell was trying to eliminate her from the DNC. President Truman had previously offered her Mitchell's job as the Chairman of the DNC, but she declined. India was very well respected in the party and it was likely that Mitchell felt threatened by her power. She finally did resign from the DNC altogether, but not until she tried to find an adequate replacement to handle women's issues. Several qualified women refused because they did not want to work with Mitchell. Kate Louchheim accepted the position, but only because she agreed with Mitchell that women should not be concerned about issues. Louchheim, in fact, instructed India not to talk about issues when she spoke before women's groups. India declined to follow her successor's advice.[2] India felt that she had let professional women down by not insisting on someone else for the job.

In the 1960s, the courts recognized unborn children as deserving of civil protection. Advocates for the rights of the unborn had a small victory on January 11, 1960, in *Smith* v. *Brennan*,[3] when a New Jersey court recognized that children have the right to sue for prenatal injuries. The baby in the case was born with severe deformities due to an automobile accident. The parents sued the driver of the automobile. The defendant's claim that the fetus was part of the mother and not a separate entity was overturned because they ignored basic scientific principles.

Smith overruled a 1942 case, *Stemmer* v. *Kline*,[4] in which Chief Justice Brogan wrote in his dissent that "there is a close dependence by the unborn child" and "it is not disputed today that the mother and the child are two separate entities. . . ." The court ruled against fetal rights on May 25, 1942.

In another case, the state awarded custody of an unborn child to the state. In order for the child to survive after birth it was necessary to perform a blood transfusion immediately after delivery. The family opposed the blood transfusion for religious reasons.

That same year, on November 1, Estelle Griswold, Executive Director of Planned Parenthood Connecticut, set the stage for legal access to contraceptives by opening an office to disburse contraceptives to married couples and also distribute information on how to prevent conception. The distribution of such information was in direct violation of Connecticut law. While the law was not generally enforced, Griswold was arrested on November 10, 1961. Justice Douglas wrote the opinion and the Supreme Court overturned the ruling. The courts had a long history of protecting the rights of married couples. They determined that some things are off limits and too important, such as privacy between spouses and families. Justice Douglas wrote that certain "peripheral rights" must be secured and thus invented the right to privacy in the Constitution where it didn't exist. He wrote:

> We have had many controversies over these penumbral rights of privacy and repose. These cases bear witness that the right of privacy which presses for recognition here is a legitimate one. . . . Would we allow the police to search the sacred precincts of

marital bedrooms for telltale signs of the use of contraceptives? The very idea is repulsive to the notions of privacy surrounding the marriage relationship.

Justices Black and Stewart dissented because they thought this set a dangerous precedent of shifting the balance of power from the legislative to the judicial branch. They wrote in the dissenting opinion:

> I discuss the due process and Ninth Amendment arguments together because on analysis they turn out to be the same thing — merely using different words to claim for this Court and the federal judiciary power to invalidate any legislative act which the judges find irrational, unreasonable or offensive.

On June 7, 1965, the Supreme Court ruled that contraception was legally permitted for married couples.

The baby boom ended a year later.

Widespread support for legal access to contraception did not include abortion. The Court's decision in *Griswold* reflected a general concern worldwide that population growth would overcome the world's limited resources to sustain the future population.

In 1972, the Supreme Court legalized the sale of contraception for unmarried couples. In *Eisenstadt* v. *Baird,* 405 U.W. 438, the Court struck down the Massachusetts statute that permitted the sale of contraceptives to married individuals but prohibited the sale to unmarried persons because it violated the equal protection clause of the 14th Amendment.

This was the critical case that provided the link from *Griswold* to *Roe* and thus legalized abortion. *Griswold* relied on a right of marital privacy, and by extending the protection to unmarried individuals it created the generalized right of privacy in reproductive affairs, upon which *Roe* was based.

Congress was also addressing population control. The Senate held hearings on a bill to create Offices of Populations Problems in the Department of State and the Department of Health, Education and Welfare. Senator Ernest Gruening (D-AK) introduced S. 1676. The Office of Economic Policy provided grants to 17 family-planning facilities to provide birth control under the auspices of the "war on poverty." The funds were limited to married couples only and included education, clinics, and contraceptives, and initially went to Planned Parenthood clinics. Planned Parenthood received bi-partisan support prior to their advocating abortion.

Presidents Eisenhower and Truman served as co-chairmen of an Honorary Council for Planned Parenthood of America.

President Johnson spoke in favor of federally funding birth control in his 1966 State of the Union address, and the 89th Congress expanded the number of programs to provide family planning services.

The biggest opponent of the expansion was the Catholic Church, which opposes artificial means of birth control. The Catholic faithful indicated that it wanted the church to alter its stance when a 1966 Gallup poll indicated that 56 percent of respondents supported a more lenient policy on birth control.

Meanwhile, the struggle among women for access to careers and equality continued. Jobs began to open up, but women felt they had one foot in the past and one foot in the present, and they were understandably angry. While women were given a taste of the freedom to achieve in the work force and become independent, they were pulled back to traditional roles. Gloria Steinham, for instance, who graduated from Smith College in 1956 and was a member of Phi Beta Kappa, sought a job as a reporter after graduation, but had trouble because the newspapers only wanted male reporters.

Betty Freidan's publication of *The Feminine Mystique* in 1963 argued that the perfect, happy, and satisfied life of the housewife was a deception glorified by the men in society.[5] She was asked to prepare a questionnaire for the 1942 graduating class at Smith College, the largest women's college in the United States, 15 years after they had graduated. The results portrayed a general unease among the respondents. This unease initiated her work on *The Feminine Mystique*. She theorized that since women were taught to find meaning in their spouse and families and not themselves, it cost women their identities. Furthermore, the new technologies that were supposed to make things easier for women, in fact, made them feel worthless because it made their job in the home less meaningful. Housewives who were offended by her book wanted to burn it, while women who embraced the book wanted to burn their bras. Either way, women increased their involvement in the political process and spoke out publicly for their needs.

The Equal Employment Opportunity Commission (EEOC) formed when Congressman Smith proposed to add sex discrimination to the Civil Rights Act of 1964. While his motives for sponsoring the addition were unclear, the bill passed. As a southern gentleman, he may have thought that white women deserved equality if blacks were going to be equal or perhaps he thought it would kill the bill. Martha Griffiths convinced the other women in Congress to support the bill's inclusion of sex discrimination.

The third National Conference on the State Commission on the Status of Women met in 1966. Friedan and Pauli Murray proposed a directive to the newly formed EEOC to request that they treat sex discrimination as seriously as race discrimination. The convention leaders were appalled that women would even think of sending a directive to a federal agency. Frustrated by the suppression of alternative ideas, they left and founded the National Organization of Women (NOW). The initial platform stated the intention "*to take action to bring women into full participation in the mainstream of American society now, exercising all privileges and responsibilities thereof in truly equal partnership with men.*" The platform did not reference birth control and abortion because Freidan felt the issues were too controversial and would detract from their goal. She believed the focus should be on enforcing current laws to address the sex discrimination in society.

In 1967, NOW changed its goals to focus on abortion and the Equal Rights Amendment (ERA). This move alienated many religious leaders and women who wanted to focus on economic and legal advances for women. This group left to form the Women's Equity Action League.

The 2006 NOW platform states that access to abortion is a matter of life or death for women. This focus on abortion brought the women's movement to a halt. In 2000, the Women's Center for Advancement commissioned a study to determine how to re-start the women's movement.[6] The study found that abortion caused so much disagreement among women that it could never be the basis for a united movement. However, there exists almost universal support among women across ethnic, age, educational achievement, and economic classes for equal pay for equal work, affordable childcare, opposition to sexual and physical abuse, and quality health care. NOW's current and almost sole focus on abortion and reproductive rights also interferes with its original goal to achieve true equality for women.

NOW should be doing more to unite women against comments like those of Senator Rick Santorum. In his recent book, *It Takes a Family: Conservatism and the Common Good,* he suggested that women should stay home and take care of their children. He ignores the fact that a vast majority of America cannot afford to have one parent stay home and, if they can, in some instances it might be more economical for the father, not the mother, to stay home. For example, if the mother worked for an engineering firm earning a high salary and the father served in the underpaid profession of teaching, the family might benefit from a higher salary and the father may choose to stay home or choose a job that allowed him to be home more.

Thirty-seven million people are living in poverty.[7] Many fathers have abandoned their families and refuse to pay child support, putting women and children in poverty. Our resources would be better used to address those kinds of situations rather than to tell moms they should stay home or simply trying to make abortion illegal without addressing the roots of the problem.

As NOW lost its momentum, Betty Freiden turned her leadership skills to growing the acceptance for abortion. Dr. Bernard N. Nathanson, Larry Lader, and Betty Friedan founded the National Association for the Repeal of Abortion Laws, which later changed its name to the National Abortion Rights Action League (NARAL). Dr. Nathanson reasoned that denying abortion was "an affront to women and a deprivation of their civil rights."[8]

Dr. Nathanson later changed his stance on abortion. He served as the director of the Center for Reproductive and Sexual Health, the largest abortion clinic in the United States. After abortion was legalized in New York, he founded the non-profit center and paid doctors $40 per hour to perform abortions. In 1974, Dr. Bernard Nathanson realized that life in the womb could not be ignored.[9] Ultrasound photos made it very clear. He produced a film, *Silent Scream and Eclipse of Reason*, showing the baby during an abortion. He also admitted the number of deaths cited by the pro-choice lobby were false. He was "deeply troubled" by his "own increasing certainty that" he "had in fact presided over 60,000 deaths." He further stated, "There is no longer serious doubt in my mind that human life exists within the womb from the very onset of pregnancy."

Even though the pro-choice lobby has been so linked to the Democratic Party, they have unwittingly helped the Republican Party because they shared the mission, in the seventies, of promoting individual liberty and limited government. The Republican Party and the pro-choice movement sought to portray the government as the enemy and fought to keep the government out of the bedroom. Since the Reagan years, the Republican mission has split within the party, though some still believe that the government should stay out of the bedroom except for homosexual relationships and abortion issues.

The pro-choice community played a role in discouraging pro-life Democrats from running by focusing their organizing efforts on the grassroots Democratic Party level. They helped make it easy for pro-life Republicans to win seats formerly held by pro-life Democrats. They also made it easy for the Republican Party to label all Democrats as supporters of abortion on demand and led Democratic women to believe that they could not be feminists and pro-life.

In 1972, the NOW leadership began a campaign to purge all pro-life women from their organization. They ignored the founders of the women's rights movement, who thought that abortion was not empowering for women, nor would it lead to equal rights. Pat Goltz's membership to NOW was canceled after the president of her local chapter told her that her pro-life advocacy conflicted with their mission. Goltz later founded Feminists for Life. Pro-life feminist Karen Lorene Ahern recalls that the local NOW chapter changed meeting places without informing her of the change once they discovered she was pro-life.

While NOW was excluding pro-life members, San Diego Bishop Leo T. Maher was denying the sacrament to NOW members because of their support for abortion.[10] Abortion-supporting women would deliberately wear their NOW buttons to mass only to be denied the sacrament. Bishop Maher explained that he was not excommunicating NOW members or abortion rights supporters, he was asking that Catholics "practice their faith." He further encouraged attendance and participation in the "life of the church."

Psychologist Irving Janis defined groupthink theory in 1972 as "a mode of thinking that people engage in when they are deeply involved in a cohesive in-group, when the members' strivings for unanimity override their motivation to realistically appraise alternative courses of action." The theory applies to NOW's decision to exclude pro-life feminists from their organization. The leaders of the organization wrongly assumed that women who opposed abortion would not be helpful in the fight to achieve equality for women. They also formed the opinion that if people did not support abortion rights, they did not support gaining true equal rights for women. They thought that women could not be pro-women and anti-abortion.

Feminists for Life was founded in 1972 to provide a home for pro-life feminists, many of whom had been excluded from the National Organization for Women because of their pro-life views. They carry on the early feminist's tradition of protecting life and advancing the rights of women. Their "Women Deserve Better" than abortion campaign reflects their message.

Endnotes

1. Betty Friedan, *The Feminine Mystique* (New York: Norton, 1963).
2. India Edwards, *Pulling No Punches: Memoirs of a Woman in Politics* (Toronto: Longman Canada Limited, 1977).
3. Supreme Court of New Jersey, 31 N.J. 353; 157A2d 497.
4. 128 N.J.L. 455 (E. & A. 1942).

5. Friedan, *The Feminine Mystique.*

6. See www.advancewomen.org.

7. Current Population Survey (CPS), 2005 Annual Social and Economic Supplement (ASEC).

8. Bernard M. Nathanson, M.D., *About Issues* (March 1989).

9. Nick Thimmesch, "Deep Doubts on Abortion," *The Progress,* Pennsylvania (December 9, 1974).

10. Nick Thimmesch, *The Progress,* Clearfield Curwensville, Philipsburg, Moshannon Valley, PA, May 9, 1975, p. 4.

CHAPTER 5

Unjust War

> "I see an interlocking directorate of death that binds the whole culture; that is an unspoken agreement that we will solve our problems by killing people, a declaration that certain people are expendable. A decent society should no more have an abortion clinic than the Pentagon." — Daniel Berrigan, S.J.

The 1968 discussion in the Democratic Party included honest and open debate about civil rights and Vietnam, and reflected the politics of the time. The Democratic Party maintained a big tent willing to debate the important issues of the day within their caucus. However, in 1968 it started down the road of silencing members of its own party. There was a fork in the road, and the pro-choice advocates forced the pro-life Democrats down the road less taken.

In 1968, a young Lieutenant John Kerry was serving his first tour in Vietnam. As a presidential candidate in 2004, he would echo the sentiment of 1968 presidential candidate Senator Eugene McCarthy, who also voted for an unjust war before he voted against it. McCarthy voted in support of a resolution that would eventually allow President Johnson to expand the war in Vietnam. He was now running on a strong anti-war platform. The Children's Crusade, anti-war college-age kids who shaved their heads and beards, campaigned as "Clean for Gene." On March 12, 1967, McCarthy did well in the New Hampshire primary, winning 42 percent of the vote to Johnson's 49 percent. Johnson announced that he did not intend to seek a second term 19 days later. The Democratic Party was clearly divided on the war in Vietnam, similar to the way the party is divided on abortion today.

A young journalist, Mark Shields, joined Senator Bobby Kennedy's campaign and witnessed the Kennedy campaign's emerging strength.[1] Kennedy united working class blacks and whites behind him and favored withdrawing from Vietnam, but he was not as outspoken as Eugene McCarthy in his stance. His candidacy was looking promising until the tragic day in June when he was murdered shortly after winning the California primary. His supporters then drifted to Humphrey, even though many of them opposed the war.

After Kennedy was assassinated, the race focused on Humphrey and McCarthy. Humphrey, who supported the war in Vietnam, held a solid majority even though he had not entered a single primary. Since the party leaders ultimately had control and chose the nominee, Humphrey was able to win because he was Johnson's heir apparent. Even though activist Democrats opposed the war, the party leadership still supported the war.

The convention delegates, who controlled the party, were chosen before the presidential candidates were even announced. It was a very closed process. Mark Shields recalls that in St. Louis, the Democrats held the convention delegate meetings on a bus, so if you were not on the bus, you could not be part of the process. Another party leader held delegate meetings in the basement of his house and locked the door so people who didn't agree with their position would not be able to participate.[2] The few in power were in touch with the rest of the country. In 1968, the rank and file public still supported the war. The country had not yet turned against the war, and the party leaders reflected that mood. The anti-war activists would later mobilize to make sure that in 1972 the control would be taken away from the party leaders. The real change occurred when the draft was instituted and after anti-war riots at Kent State University in Ohio in 1970.

The 1968 Convention saw a deeply divided party. Anti-war protesters, who were highly organized and vocal, wanted to be heard. Chicago Mayor Richard Daley wanted to maintain peace in his city and prepared for the anti-war protesters. He prepared a war zone. Police were on every corner, the National Guard was given a "shoot to kill" order, the convention hall was surrounded by a barbed wire fence, and bullet-proof glass was installed at the entrance. The stifling heat and the unreliable air conditioners resulted in short tempers.[3] The protesters ranged from People Against Racism to The Lutheran Action Committee to the Women's Peace Group, and some had every intention of provoking the police. When a curfew was ignored on the Sunday before the convention began, the police could not control the crowds, and rioting ensued outside the convention hall.

While the non-delegates were protesting outside the convention hall, the delegates argued vociferously inside the convention hall about the war. There were walkouts, demands for immediate withdrawal, and demands to immediately stop the bombing. The anti-war forces did not have the majority, yet their voices were heard inside the hall. Even with the negative press focused on attempts to silence the protesters outside the convention hall, a majority of the people agreed with how the city handled the situation. A 1968 poll showed that a majority of blue-collar workers supported the way the police handled the protesters.[4]

These were troubled times and the party needed a strong voice to unite it. In his acceptance speech, Humphrey said, "It is the special genius of the Democratic Party that it welcomes change, not as an enemy but as an ally . . . not as a force to be suppressed, but as an instrument of progress to be encouraged. This week our party has debated the great issues before America in this very hall. Had we not raised these issues, troublesome as they were, we would have ignored the reality of change."[5]

The party met the challenge of a great controversy with discussion, albeit heated, and dialogue, not silence. While Humphrey did his best to unite the party, it was too late for the presidential race. The Republican Party had united behind Nixon and was able to defeat Humphrey. However, the Democrats were able to maintain control over both the House and the Senate.

The convention approved a minority report to reform the nominating process. Senator McGovern's reform efforts ultimately gave abortion rights supporters a larger voice within the party. The McGovern/Fraser Commission included Birch Bayh, Senator George Mitchell, Warren Christopher, and other future leaders of the Democratic Party. They concluded that increasing the number of primaries would allow more freedom in choosing delegates, and put more power in the hands of the people, a much more democratic process. In 1968, less than one-third of states held presidential primaries, and 12 million people voted. Four years later, the number of primaries jumped from 9 to 35. In 1972, 22 million people participated.

The 1972 reforms resulted in activists having more control over the platform and nominations than elected officials. This change has resulted in candidates and positions that favor the views of the activist fringes and not the majority position of the public. For example, polls have shown increasing favor among the public for some restrictions on abortion, but the Democratic Party removed from its platform a recognition of pro-life views within the party.

Endnotes

1. Interview with Mark Shields, December 6, 2005.
2. Rhodes Cook, "The Nominating Process," *Congressional Quarterly*, p. 43.
3. Haynes Johnson, "Return to Chicago," *Washington Post*, August 25, 1996.
4. Paul F. Boller, *Presidential Campaigns* (New York and Oxford: Oxford University Press, 1996).
5. Hubert Humphrey, acceptance speech: A New Day for America, August 29, 1968, Chicago, IL.

CHAPTER 6

ERA and Abortion

"The sexual politics that disturbed the sense of priorities of the women's movement during the 1970s made it easy for the so-called moral majority to lump ERA with homosexual rights and abortion into one explosive package of licentious, family-threatening sex."
— Betty Friedan

Women secured access to contraception, but still found they had not achieved equality with their male counterparts. They were still being paid less than men, there were fewer women in management positions, and there were fewer opportunities. The Equal Rights Amendment, which had stagnated, began to regain momentum.

The ERA had been reintroduced in 1967, but failed to gain enough support and was stalled in the male-dominated Congress. In 1970, Congresswoman Martha Griffiths petitioned the Judiciary Committee to release H.J.Res. 264, which would provide equal rights for women, and move it to the floor for a vote. A "discharge petition" is used when a majority of legislators disagree with a committee chairman or House leadership hold on a bill and would like to see a vote on the legislation. It requires 218 signatures. The Equal Rights Amendment passed after only an hour debate, by a 352 to 15 vote.

Senator Eugene McCarthy (D-MN) introduced the companion bill in the Senate. The Senate Judiciary Committee held hearings on the bill and the Senate debated the measure in October of 1970. Senator Sam Ervin (D-NC) introduced an amendment to exempt women from military service, which passed by a vote of 36 to 33. Many thought the amendment was an attempt to kill the bill, and it succeeded because senators were split on women serving in the military. Because it exempted women from military service, ERA supporters opposed this version of the bill. The Senate did not vote on the measure that year.

The ERA was reintroduced and H.J. Res. 208 passed again in 1971 by a 354 to 24 vote in the House. The Senate passed the legislation in 1972 by a vote of 84 to 8. The deadline for ratification was 1979.

The author of the 1921 ERA, Alice Paul, opposed abortion and called it "the ultimate exploitation of women." Yet the two issues became linked after *Roe* v. *Wade* was decided. Advocates for abortion rights were split on the linking of the two, but once joined it was almost impossible to look at the issues separately. Author Jane Mansbridge recalls that the "conservative activities saw abortion and the ERA as two prongs of the libbers general strategy for undermining traditional American values."[1]

In 1978, the Supreme Court ruled, in *Hawaii Right to Life* v. *Chang*, that denying funds for abortion did not violate the equal protection clause, a major defeat for the American Civil Liberties Union (ACLU) who was making the claim.

A few years later, in 1980, the Court ruled in favor of protecting potential life. The opinion, written by Justice Stewart, upheld the restrictions on funding abortion in *Harris* v. *McRae*. The Court further ruled that the Social Security Act, which authorized the Medicaid program, did not require that states pay for abortion. Justices Brennan, Marshall, Blackmun, and Stevens dissented.

A year later, the abortion rights movement claimed a victory in *Moe* v. *the Secretary of Administration*, when the Massachusetts Supreme Court ruled that the restrictions on funding abortion violated the due process clause of the Massachusetts Constitution. Several states followed suit but struck down the ERA/abortion claim even though some thought it had merit.

When Speaker Thomas P. "Tip" O'Neill brought the Equal Rights Amendment to the floor in 1983 under the suspension of the rules, the effort failed. Unanimous consent is usually reserved for non-controversial bills because only 40 minutes of debate is allowed, no amendments are allowed, and the bill can only pass with a two-thirds majority. The effort failed.

Earlier in the year, the Judiciary Committee had held hearings on H.J.Res. 1. The tenor of the hearings had changed considerably since 1972. The new focus was on how the ERA would affect abortion policy. The partisan split widened as well. While the ERA previously had tremendous bi-partisan support and the proponents and opponents were not split on a partisan level, the 1983 vote enjoyed overwhelming support from Democrats (225-38) and opposition from Republicans (53-109).

That same year, a Bureau of Labor Statistics report was released on women in poverty, and the U.S. Civil Rights Commission released a report on "A Growing Crisis: Disadvantaged Women and Their Children" showing that there was a 54 percent increase in women-headed households living in poverty. By contrast, the number of poor families led by men dropped by 50 percent. The Democrat-led Congress tried to address the issue by introducing legislation to help women obtain jobs and provide childcare for low-income women.

As Friedan stated, and many agreed, the ERA failed to gain the necessary support because of the abortion issue. Pro-life groups vehemently opposed the ERA after the Pennsylvania Supreme Court ruled against denying Medicaid funds for abortion because it violated the state's ERA. Years later, after the ERA failed to achieve ratification by the states, Freidan blamed the loss on the National Organization of Women, with whom she had parted ways several years earlier. "The sexual politics that disturbed the sense of priorities of the women's movement during the 1970s made it easy for the so-called moral majority to lump the ERA with homosexual rights and abortion into one explosive package of licentious, family-threatening sex."[2]

The abortion/ERA link has continued to be an obstacle to passing a national ERA, and states continue to accept the link. In 1998, the New Mexico Supreme Court ruled that the State ERA mandated that the state pay for abortions.

The ERA had failed, but abortion rights advocates were making progress.

In June of 1967, abortion rights supporters had their first victory when Colorado passed legislation to legalize abortion in cases of rape, incest, physical or mental health, or fetal abnormality. Abortion had been a felony in most cases in 49 states and the District of Columbia. In 42 states, abortion was legal only to save the life of the mother. Other states allowed abortion to "save a woman from serious and permanent bodily harm, life, or health."[3] Alaska, Hawaii, and Washington had no penalties for abortion in the early stages of pregnancy, but required a licensed physician to perform the procedure. Twelve states, Arkansas, Delaware, Georgia, Kansas, Maryland, Mississippi, New Mexico, North Carolina, Oregon, South Carolina, and Virginia, passed restrictive laws allowing abortion only for pregnancies due to assault, rape, incest, to save the life of the mother, or for severe fetal handicap. The District of Columbia and 13 other states permitted abortion under certain circumstances, and at least 30 states considered new abortion legislation. The courts had ruled in favor of access to abortion in Illinois and California.[4] Abortion rights supporters were making progress and the backing of a major political party would help their cause. By 1972, the Democratic Party was ready to accept the offer.

The state of New York passed the first abortion law that did not have restrictions until 24-weeks. Assemblyman Al Blumenthal, a supporter of Senator Robert Kennedy, introduced the legislation. When asked about his position on abortion, Senator Robert Kennedy didn't answer.[5] Republican Governor Nelson Rockefeller signed the legislation. Rockefeller was a real conservative who did not have concern for the little guy and supported corporations. He was governor during the

Attica uprising. Two years later, the legislature repealed the abortion law. However, the abortion law remained in effect because Governor Rockefeller vetoed the repeal.

California passed legislation with an extremely loose interpretation of "mental health," thereby essentially allowing abortion on demand.

In the 1970s, party was not a predictor on how one would vote on abortion. However, many of the leaders in the pro-life movement were Republican. There were exceptions. Republican Governor and future President of the United States Ronald Reagan signed the California bill legalizing abortion into law. Ten years later, and after a change in heart on abortion, he was able to seduce pro-life Democrats to vote for him. His prior views on abortion had been safely tucked away.

The legislative process was working and states were debating the issues. Washington state passed a referendum to allow the voters the opportunity to decide if abortion should be legalized. The state House passed a bill legalizing abortion by a vote of 64 to 31 with the support of 25 Democrats. The vote on Referendum 20 occurred on November 3, 1970, and was approved by a 51 to 49 percent margin. Michigan followed suit in 1972 and voted 61 to 39 percent against legalizing abortion. North Dakota voted 78 to 22 percent against legalizing abortion.

In 1971, President Nixon vetoed the Comprehensive Child Development Act that would authorize federally funded day care. Nixon thought that it was "fiscally irresponsible."[6] The legislation would have provided for the education, nutrition, and health care needs of low-income children. Middle-income children would have been eligible for the program but charged a fee. Minnesota Senator Fritz Mondale sponsored the childcare initiative and called the veto "totally indefensible."

The Administration tried to reduce the number of students eligible for the school lunch program by first decreasing the reimbursement rate and then by trying to increase eligibility standards. Forty-one Democrats, joined by 18 Republicans, wrote to President Nixon urging him to cancel the "eligibility standards."[7]

The Democrats continued to advocate for protections for all. However, we were about to turn a corner.

Endnotes

1. Jane Mansbrige, *Why We Lost the ERA* (Chicago, IL: The University of Chicago Press, 1986).

2. Moira Davison Reynolds, *Women Advocates of Reproductive Rights: Eleven Who Led the Struggle in the United States and Britain* (Jefferson, NC and London: McFarland & Co., Inc., 1994).

3. Francois B. Gerard, *Abortion — Murder or Mercy? Analysis and Bibliography* (Huntington, NY: Nova Science Publishers, Inc., 2001).

4. *Oakland Tribune,* July 24, 1972.

5. Thomas Maier, *The Kennedys, America's Emerald Kings* (New York: Basic Books, 2003).

6. *Congressional Quarterly Almanac,* 1971, page 504.

7. *Congressional Quarterly Almanac,* 1971, p. 499.

CHAPTER 7

Acid, Amnesty, and Abortion

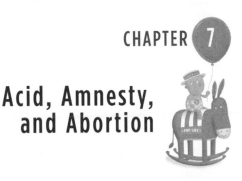

"We just got beat by the cast of *Hair*." — Speaker of the House Tip O'Neil of McGovern's primary victory

In 1972, Senator George McGovern ran as the Democratic candidate for president on an anti-war platform. McGovern, a true progressive, served in World War II as a bomber pilot. In the U.S. House for 2 terms (1957 to 1961) and the U.S. Senate for 18 years (1963 to 1981), he led efforts to transform the nation's food programs, including forming the Women, Infants and Children and School Lunch programs. He recalls watching a CBS documentary about hunger in the United States with his daughter in 1968. The report showed a little boy with his head hung low and ashamed because he didn't have any money for food.[1] President Kennedy appointed McGovern as the first head of the Food for Peace Program. In 1997, he served as the U.S. Permanent Representative to the United Nation's Food and Agriculture Organization.

Discontent with the war was growing and carried the McGovern campaign. His 1968 reforms included a quota system that brought more young people and women to the party and built support for his anti-war campaign. The reforms also brought in a heavier dose of young liberal activists. Women delegates increased from 13 percent in 1968 to 40 percent in 1972. Most of the women supported abortion,[2] and they knew how the platform system worked because of their activism in the anti-war movement. These women delegates spearheaded an effort to add an abortion plank to the platform. The effort was defeated because McGovern opposed an abortion plank. He knew that adding abortion to the Democratic platform would hurt him against Nixon.

In the debate on the abortion language, a platform committee member stated, "We can't be known as the abortion party." McGovern called abortion reform a "no win issue" and said that these decisions should be left up to the states.

McGovern's first choice for the vice president slot was Senator Thomas Eagleton of Missouri, a Catholic pro-life Democrat. When Eagleton stepped down over allegations about his mental health, McGovern chose another Catholic pro-life Democrat, Sargent Shriver, to serve as his vice president. The pro-choice forces had not yet gained strength enough to ban qualified candidates from achieving higher office and maintaining a pro-life position. However, Shriver's wife's anti-abortion position was cited as a reason to not select him.[3] Eunice Kennedy Shriver, the sister of John F. Kennedy, proved to be a strong force on the campaign trail, and she avoided discussing how she and McGovern disagreed on the abortion issue. She simply said, "I don't

see that my attitude toward abortion is relative to the Mc-
Govern campaign."

Mr. Shriver would later be criticized for his pro-life
position and his wife's strong and outspoken pro-life position. However, Mrs. Shriver has remained a consistent voice
against abortion. In 1967, at a Birthright meeting, she called
for one million families to adopt "unwanted" babies. In the
"One Million for Life" program, she wanted to show mothers with unplanned pregnancies that adoption was a better
choice and that their children were wanted.[4] Mrs. Shriver
continued to be a strong advocate for the unborn. That same
year she sponsored a conference on abortion and warned that
using abortion to prevent mental retardation could result
in scientists deciding who should live and who should die.
Scientists could eventually be charged with allowing only
those with the proper genes to procreate and "do away with
the people over 65 who are ill and tired of living."[5]

In response to the *Casey* v. *Planned Parenthood* ruling,
Eunice Kennedy Shriver wrote that she thought they had
overlooked something in the ruling. They spoke about "the
rights of women and the rights of states," but there was nothing about "the rights of the infant in the womb." She further
wrote about our country's long history of "defending the
defenseless" and opening our doors to immigrants, helping
the homeless, the handicapped, and the elderly, and said that
"we cannot exclude infants from the human community."
She encouraged everyone to reduce abortion and declared
that the best solution was to "eliminate the need."

Even though the party did not include abortion in its platform, vocal anti-war pro-abortion rights activists unknowingly

helped the Republicans use it against Democrats in the 1972 campaign and thus began a 30-year campaign during which Republicans have used the abortion issue against the Democrats. McGovern supported abortion but thought it should not be part of our platform. Spiro Agnew defined Democrats as the party of amnesty (for draft dodgers), acid (legalized drugs), and abortion, which effectively ended McGovern's chances for the presidency. Humphrey was desperate to win the nomination and echoed Spiro Agnew's words.

Nixon and the Republicans were reaching out to the Catholic vote, a natural constituency of the Democratic Party. Nixon solidified the support from the pro-life community by appearing with Terence Cardinal Cooke, archbishop of New York, to express his support for the Catholic position against abortion. Nixon said, "In this firm stand with your millions of fellow Roman Catholics whose dogma properly abhors laws giving the states the right to condemn to the death living souls in their mothers' wombs by indiscriminate abortion. . . ."[6]

The McGovern reforms truly changed the voice and message of the Democratic Party. Former mayor of Boston and ambassador to the Vatican Ray Flynn recalls that there were over 1,025 people interested in being honorary delegates to the 1968 Democratic Convention. In 1972, delegates were selected early so that only four people showed up at the meeting and only one person could be selected as a delegate. Ambassador Flynn believes that these reforms killed the party. Instead of mainstream social and economic justice delegates, we had delegates fighting to include abortion on demand, gay rights, and other issues.

After serving as Boston's mayor, Flynn served as the ambassador to the Vatican from 1993–1997. He ran for a congressional seat in 1998, and many attribute the loss to his pro-life stance. Flynn believes that lawmakers make decisions on their best political interest. Many of his friends have said, "Thank you so much for your support over the years, but I can't be pro-life or the special interest organizations will not support me, and I want to win." Flynn maintains that when you run as a pro-life Democrat, you run on your own. Politicians are savvy and know that all they have to do is be pro-choice and they will get financial support. In places like Boston, most of the politicians would prefer to be pro-life, but candidates need money to win.[7]

The 1972 convention was televised, and portrayed the Democratic Party as the party of homosexual rights, abortion rights, amnesty for draft dodgers, and other liberal causes. Former Speaker of the House Tip O'Neill, who was disappointed with McGovern's nomination, had supported Senator Ed Muskie. Summing up the primary defeat, he said, "We just got beat by the cast of *Hair*." Congressman James O'Hara summed up the effects of the convention and the reforms: "The American people made an association today between McGovern and gay liberation and welfare rights and pot-smoking and black militants and women's lib and wise college kids." Liberal became a dirty word.

Endnotes

1. George McGovern, *The Essential America, Our Founders and the Liberal Tradition* (New York: Simon & Shuster, 2004).
2. Mark Stricherz, "How a Little-known Task Force Helped Create Red State/Blue State America," *Boston Globe*, November 23, 2004.

3. *New York Times*, August 6, 1972, p. 28, col. 1.

4. "Mrs. Shriver Outspoken," *The Sheboygan Press*, August 9, 1972.

5. "Abortion Change Perils Cited by Mrs. Shriver," New York Times Service, *Syracuse Herald-Journal*, September 9, 1967.

6. *The News*, Frederick, Maryland, May 20, 1972.

7. Interview with Ray Flynn.

CHAPTER  8

The Doctors' Right to Choose

"There is no absolute right to do with one's body what you like." — Justice Harry Blackmun, author of *Roe* v. *Wade*.

On January 22, 1973, Senator and Chairman of the Human Resources Committee Bill Gluba, a pro-life Democrat, held a hearing on a bill to legalize abortion in Iowa. Two Republican Senators, Minet Dotter and Phil Hill, had introduced the measure. Senator Gluba knew in advance that the vote to legalize abortion would fail in committee by a vote of eight to three but wanted to be fair and to let voices be heard. Bill says he remembers this day like it was yesterday. At precisely 2:15, the secretary of the Senate walked in and said the hearing was over because "you no longer have jurisdiction over the issue. Abortion is now the law of the land." Gluba expressed the opinion, and many agreed, that the Supreme Court legislated on this issue. They didn't hold hearings and they didn't listen to voters or the will of the American people.

The road to legal abortion began in 1973, when an unmarried pregnant woman challenged an 1854 Texas statute that prohibited abortion. The original intent of *Roe* v. *Wade* was to show the unconstitutionality of the Texas law that criminalized the conduct of doctor and/or women involved in an abortion. Legal scholars on both sides of the issue and at both ends of the political spectrum agree that *Roe* v. *Wade* is a poorly written decision. Even abortion rights supporters think that *Roe* was a poor legal decision and that Blackmun could have crafted a ruling with a stronger legal foundation. However, the young justice had tremendous respect for the medical community and was provided much leeway in drafting his decision.

The Supreme Court decided that it was unconstitutional for abortion to be criminalized, prohibited states from making abortion a crime, and prohibited states from making access to abortion difficult. It also introduced the concept of viability, and defined viability as the point at which the fetus can survive outside the womb. The decision was based on the earlier *Griswold* decision that created the right to privacy for married couples. However, the *Roe* decision was not limited only to married couples.

Justice Blackmun, who authored the decision, claimed that he never intended to allow abortion on demand, to give women "an absolute right to abortion," or to "compel abortion on demand." Blackmun had faith in and respect for doctors and provided them with the right to determine if a woman needed an abortion. He believed that doctors would perform abortions only in medically necessary situations. *Roe* v. *Wade* states that abortion "must be left to the medical judgment of the pregnant woman's attending physician." Today, the "medically necessary situation" has become very broad, and many abortion doctors are willing to perform an abortion for any reason.

After ruling on criminality, the *Roe* decision went to great lengths to define the viability of an unborn child. Determining the viability of an unborn child was much different in 1973 and that determination may yet change in the coming years with further advances in medical science. The Court voted seven to two in favor of protecting the right to abortion.

Roe prohibited states from considering a fetus a person. Therefore, the fetus did not have a right to life. It did not prevent states from passing laws to protect the child from harm, however, and states have passed laws to acknowledge that a fetus can feel pain. A person can be charged with a crime if he or she hurts an unborn child.

The recent fights over filling the vacancies on the Supreme Court have made the history of abortion decisions by the Supreme Court rather interesting. Justice Harry Blackmun, appointed by Republican President Richard Nixon, wrote the ill-fated decision. At the time of the *Roe* v. *Wade* decision, there were only three Democratic appointees. On the Court, Thurgood Marshall, who was appointed by Johnson, and William Douglas, who was appointed by Roosevelt, supported *Roe*. The other, Justice Byron White, who was appointed by Democratic President John Kennedy, voted against *Roe* and became one of its leading critics.

Only one of the six Republican appointed Justices, William Renquist, who was later elevated to Chief Justice, voted against the decision.

Justice	Appointed by
Douglas, William Orville** (for)	Roosevelt
Brennan, William J., Jr. (for)	Eisenhower
Stewart, Potter (for)	Eisenhower
Marshall, Thurgood** (for)	Johnson
Powell, Lewis F., Jr. (for)	Nixon
Renquist, William H. (against)	Nixon
Blackmun, Harry A. (for)	Nixon
Burger, Warren* (for)	Nixon
White, Byron Raymond** (against)	Kennedy

  * indicates Chief Justice

  ** indicates Democrat appointee

Roe disrupted the legislative process and the formation of a national consensus. It was not done incrementally nor was it allowed to evolve slowly over time. Instead of allowing the nation to debate on the issue that had started in the states, *Roe* stopped the process. The result of the decision caused people to take sides, either pro-choice or pro-life, and 30 years later there is still no resolution. *Roe* is the symbol, main argument, and main fundraising piece for both sides. Changing public opinion happens at its own speed, and 30 years later we are still debating the abortion issue, but public opinion is turning to view abortion as morally wrong. Columnist Richard Cohen wrote in an October 20, 2005, *Washington Post* column, "I no longer see abortion as directly related to sexual freedom or feminism, and I no longer see it strictly as a matter of personal privacy, either. It entails questions about life — maybe more so at the end of the process than at the beginning, but life nonetheless."

Shortly after the *Roe* v. *Wade* decision, Senator Harold Hughes (D) and Senator Mark Hatfield (R) cosponsored a Human Life Amendment to protect life from conception. Both men were considered anti-war progressives. In a June 21, 1973, article, Jeffery Hart discussed fetal development as described by Dr. A.W. Liley, a professor of fetal physiology. Hart expressed confidence that the Human Life Amendment would pass because "from Dr. Liley's description one gains a fresh sense of the reality of just how early recognizable human life appears."[1] Sadly, he was wrong. It took the advent of the ultrasound machine and people being able to see the babies to begin a change in public opinion.

In 1974, Ella Grasso was elected as governor of Connecticut, defeating Robert Steele in an open-seat contest. She was re-elected to a second four-year term in 1978 in hotly contested campaigns in both the primary and general election. She was the first woman governor of her state as well as the first woman governor of any state elected in her own right.

Grasso won despite the National Women's Political Caucus endorsement of her pro-choice male opponent. She was an advocate for the Equal Rights Amendment, but was opposed to abortion. A NOW official called her attitude "typical of her lack of understanding of feminism and its objectives."[2] Grasso held firm on her pro-life position, stating, "I'm opposed to abortion because I happen to believe that life deserves the protection of society." Once elected governor, she prohibited the state from using Medicaid funds to pay for abortion, citing that she did not want to "be a party to killing the children of the poor."[3] A Great Society liberal, she served as the first woman floor leader in the Connecticut House of Representatives. She served on the Democratic National Committee from 1956–1958 and as the co-chairman of the 1960 Democratic National Convention.[4]

Some in the pro-life community refer to the Supreme Court in this era as the "death court." A year after *Roe* v. *Wade*, the Supreme Court legalized the death penalty. The Supreme Court also ruled that states couldn't require a woman seeking an abortion to get consent from her husband or force teenage girls to get consent from a parent.

Endnotes

1. Jeffery Hart, "Human Life Amendment," *Ironwood Daily Globe*, June 21, 1973.
2. *Syracuse Herald-Journal*, October 24, 1975, p. 2.
3. Lise Stone, "Ex-Connecticut Governor Dies — Grasso Always Modest about Role," *Syracuse Hearald-Journal*, February 6, 1981.
4. Susan Ella Bysiewicz, *A Biography of Governor Ella Grasso* (Old Saybrook, CT: Peregrine Press, 1984).

CHAPTER 9

A Failure of Leadership

> "Abortion is put forth as a solution for the poor, but I think the poor want better housing, more jobs and food on their tables. I don't think aborting their babies makes them any happier. I think it probably contributes to their misery." — Ellen McCormack

Many believe that the 1992 campaign was the first time that the pro-life position was an issue for Democrats. However, pro-life Democrat leaders have tried to promote a pro-life position in the party since the abortion debate began.

In 1976, the leader was the daughter of Irish immigrants, housewife, and mother of four, Ellen McCormack from New York. Before marrying New York City policeman Jack McCormack, she served as a legal secretary. Passionately pro-life, she became the first woman to qualify for federal matching funds for a presidential race. She successfully raised $50,000 in 20 states from less than $250 per person in order to qualify for the federal matching funds. In May of 1976, she was one of few presidential candidates still eligible for the federal money because she won at least ten percent of the vote in two primaries. The other candidates were President Ford, then California Governor Ronald Reagan, Congressman Morris Udall, Congressman Scoop Jackson, and Georgia Governor Jimmy Carter.[1]

As the founder of the Right to Life of New York, she sought every opportunity to talk about life issues. At the time, television stations would not run pro-life advertisements, but as a presidential candidate and under the new campaign rules she was protected by the First Amendment for her political campaign and could run pro-life advertisements.

Many thought she wasn't making a serious effort for the presidency. In an interview at the 1976 convention she replied, "The fact that I am unprofessional and we had to work with a grassroots level probably gives us a different image. But it doesn't mean that I wasn't serious. And my prime issue was to speak out in defense of the unborn. And I became a candidate because the other candidates would not speak out on the defense of the unborn."

When questioned about her single issue candidacy and the importance of all the other issues, she replied "If [the major politicians] can't understand that every human being has a right to life then they can't really stand up and talk about the poor and the problems of budget. And they can't deal with international situations because it is dealing with humanity, and if they can ignore the tiniest human being just because they can't see them, I don't believe they can solve the other problems."[2]

A political novice and pro-life Democrat decided to run as a delegate for McCormack. He took time off from a paying job to work to elect Steve Foley who ran on the plank "Put Life in the Democratic Party." The young volunteer recalls that fellow Democrats treated them very disrespectfully. He further recalls that no one would listen to the candidate's pro-life position and that they were "treated like lepers." Even after the experience, he wanted to continue to be active in politics. After the election, he decided to join the local Democratic Club. Unfortunately, pro-life Democrats were not welcome. Even so, this young political activist had caught the political bug. He became the executive director of the New Jersey Right to Life Committee and in 1977 he testified at a hearing on national health insurance in support of health care for everyone from the unborn children to seniors.

A report was made at the request of HHS Secretary Califano. As the leader for the People Expressing A Concern for Everyone (PEACE), he was arrested for a peaceful sit-in at an abortion clinic. He had modeled his style after leaders Martin Luther King and Mohandas Gandhi, but all charges were dropped, depriving him of an opportunity to use the "necessity" defense: that it was "necessary" to trespass to prevent a killing or many killings at the abortion clinic. He decided he would run for office. He had grown up a Democrat. His father was a teamster. He was a strong supporter of worker rights and safety, protecting the environment, and other Democrat values. He worked on Democrat campaigns. How could he be anything but a Democrat?

The day of the filing deadline, he changed his party affiliation and ran as a Republican because the Democrat Party wouldn't support him unless he agreed to change his position. Republican Congressman Chris Smith was elected to serve in the United States Congress in 1981, where he has been one of the strongest leaders and driving forces on pro-life legislation — from conception to natural death. He has been a strong advocate for human rights worldwide, has helped victims of religious repression and torture, and has authored three historic laws to combat sex trafficking. He has fought for better education and health care benefits for veterans and has been a leader in fighting against sexual predators of children. He should be a Democrat.

Other candidates for president in 1976 included California Governor Edmund Brown, Congressman Morris Udall, Sargent Shriver, Birch Bayh, and Scoop Jackson. Although Shriver had a longstanding pro-life record, Dr. Mildred Jefferson of the National Right to Life Committee didn't believe that his record was strong enough because he didn't oppose *Roe* and would not support a human life amendment. Shriver's campaign manager, Teddi Nardi, said that Shriver's "Catholicism is being questioned."[3]

They were challenging a governor from the state of Georgia, Jimmy Carter, who himself was pro-life. Carter was considered an outsider to the Washington establishment, which proved to be an advantage.

As would any good candidate, Carter was trying to build support for his campaign and played to the crowds. He told Catholic and religious groups he was opposed to abortion, and women's groups that he respected their rights without endorsing abortion. To win the nomination, Carter was trying to appease both sides of the abortion debate. Sargent Shriver accused Carter of "waffling" on a "controversial issue."[4] Shriver called for major research to "develop a foolproof birth control device" to provide an "alternative to abortion."

Pro-lifers in Iowa turned out for the caucuses because they believed in this man of faith who was born again. He advocated the equal rights movement and supported diversity. He appointed the first woman to chair the convention and was nominated by Andrew Young, an African-American Democrat from Georgia.

The pro-choice camp was working hard to redefine "liberal" to exclude anyone who opposed abortion, and sent the message that if a candidate didn't support abortion, they would not support you.

Pro-choice supporters again attempted to add an abortion plank to the platform, and this time they were successful despite Carter's opposition. When the language finally passed, Carter said that he would have worded the language differently because he thinks "abortions are wrong," and "as president he would work to minimize them"[5] He further stated that he did "not support constitutional amendments to overturn the Supreme Court ruling on abortion. However, I personally disapprove of abortion . . . if within the confines of the Supreme Court ruling, we can work out legislation to minimize abortions with better family planning, adoption procedures, and contraception for those who desire it, I would favor such a law."[6]

Carter did not follow the steps of McGovern and choose a pro-life running mate. Instead, he chose Senator Fritz Mondale. Mondale helped elect Hubert Humphrey to the U.S. Senate and then served there himself. Prior to serving in the Senate, Mondale served as the attorney general of Minnesota. His strong pro-choice stance would later destroy his chances of winning the Senate seat in the 2002 election, losing to Republican Senator Norm Coleman. During a debate, Coleman invited Mondale to join him in opposing partial birth abortions and supporting parental notification — something that the vast majority of Minnesotans supported. Mondale stumbled for an answer, afraid to move from the rigid ideological position dictated by the pro-abortion forces.

While the Democrats became more entrenched with the abortion rights supporters, the Republican Party started to move in the other direction. In the mid-70s, a young conservative, Paul Weyrich, rose to leadership and started to support only pro-life Republicans. He refused to support any Republican who supported abortion. One of his first successes was Congressman Henry Hyde. He formed the Free Congress Foundation whose main focus was the culture war, and helped found the Moral Majority with Jerry Falwell.

The election was a crucial turning point for the Democratic Party, which should have sided with Carter on his goal to reduce the abortion rate by supporting programs to help women instead of fighting for the right to have an abortion. The voices of the abortion rights supporters drowned out the voices of those in the party, including Carter, who thought supporting legalized abortion on demand was not the direction the party should head.

Clardy Craven, a social worker in Minnesota, spoke at the convention against abortion. She was the second African American woman to speak at a Democratic convention. However, Carter's goal to have a middle of the road platform failed, and an abortion plank was included in the platform for the first time. It stated:

We fully recognize the religious and ethical nature of the concerns which many Americans have on the subject of abortion. We feel, however, that it is undesirable to attempt to amend the U.S. Constitution to overturn the Supreme Court decision in this area.

At the convention, Ellen McCormack and others felt betrayed by Carter, who appeared to soften his position on abortion. James Killilea of Massachusetts nominated Ms. McCormack for president. He was a reluctant speaker and thought someone else should give the speech. In his modesty, he said that he thought they chose him because of his Boston accent, but the passion and emotion is his speech could not have not been matched by another.[7]

"In officially becoming the party on abortion," he said, "the Democratic Party and Mr. X[8] are not only saying things about the party but us all. They think that a few soothing words will cool us down. They say that there are not enough of us to make any difference. Only if we prove them wrong on election day will we prove them wrong." Unfortunately, it took almost 20 years before this happened. He also cautioned that the Democratic Party had essentially "expelled Catholics" and it was equivalent to putting up signs "No Catholics Need Apply." He explained, "Although not all pro-life people are Catholic, the vast majority of Catholics are pro-life."

He accused President Carter of deceiving voters by taking a strong pro-life stance and then changing his position. He criticized Carter and his followers of not listening to McCormack, and for denying her space on the convention floor which was promised to all presidential candidates. However, not many of the delegates heard Mr. Killilea, or if they did hear, they didn't listen to his warnings. The noise from the hall was so overpowering that even those who wanted to listen could hardly hear.

People barely took notice of a quieter protest by Rev. Robert N. Deming of the Cathedral of the Immaculate Conception in Kansas City. He declined the opportunity to give the closing benediction because "he could not in good conscience give the benediction when he found himself in opposition to the abortion views of the candidate and the party."[9]

On the contrary, the Republican platform supported a constitutional amendment to ban abortions, but also included language to include pro-choice Republicans. The Republican platform stated:

> The question of abortion is one of the most difficult and controversial of our time. It is undoubtedly a moral and personal issue but it also involves complex questions relating to medical science and criminal justice. There are those in our Party who favor complete support for the Supreme Court decision which permits abortion on demand. There are others who share sincere convictions that the Supreme Court's decision must be changed by a constitutional amendment prohibiting all abortions. Others have yet to take a position, or they have assumed a stance somewhere in between polar positions.
>
> We protest the Supreme Court's intrusion into the family structure through its denial of the parents'

obligation and right to guide their minor children. The Republican Party favors a continuance of the public dialogue on abortion and supports the efforts of those who seek enactment of a constitutional amendment to restore protection of the right to life for unborn children.

The Republican Party portrayed a big tent policy that welcomed those with differing views. They began to court pro-life Democrats by sending the message that if one was truly pro-life, there was only one party that would provide welcome.

That same year, the debate on whether or not federal funds should be used to pay for abortion began to gain momentum. One evening in June, Congressman Jim Oberstar (D-MN), Congressman Henry Hyde (R-IL), Congressman Al Quie (R-MN), and Congressman Bob Bauman (R-MD) joined on the House floor to discuss federal funding of abortions. About $50 million was being spent each year in the Labor, Health and Human Services Appropriations bill to pay for abortions,[10] and the members did not agree with federal money being spent in this fashion. The members talked about limitation language, but they did not want to impose a new responsibility. Additionally, that avenue would be subject to a point of order legislating on an appropriations bill and be prohibited.

They decided on prohibitive language that would forbid federal money for abortion. Congressman Oberstar handwrote the language on the House floor with a piece of paper and a pen and passed it to the other members for editing. They made a few changes and Oberstar walked the draft over to the House parliamentarian to ensure it was in order.

The members then discussed who should offer the amendment. They thought they would have an easier time passing the legislation with a Republican co-sponsor, because a Republican, Gerald Ford, was president. Bauman was reluctant, so Hyde offered the amendment. Ford initially leaned toward vetoing the legislation until Democratic presidential nominee Jimmy Carter expressed his opposition to federally funded abortions.[11]

Carter implied that he and Ford's positions on abortion were identical. Once Carter made his statement, Ford agreed that he would sign the legislation if it were presented to him. He never signed the legislation and, in fact, vetoed the bill when it was presented to him. Ford defended his position by trying to hide behind the Republican platform, saying that it represented his position. He then tied Carter to the Democratic Platform. Ironically, neither candidate agreed with their prospective platforms.

Ford's position on abortion was not clear. At a reception in Concord, New Hampshire, on February 8, 1976, a reporter asked Ford if his "change of heart" with respect to *Roe* was a "political move." Ford responded that he was always "adverse to the Supreme Court decision" and it was an issue of states' rights.[12] That same day, at a Q&A session at the University of New Hampshire, he said that he did "not support the better known amendment that would preclude any abortion whatsoever" and thought there should be a balance. He later clarified that both the Supreme Court decision to make abortion on demand legal and the constitutional amendment to make it completely illegal both went too far. He thought that people "should not be bound on the one hand by a certain decision of the Supreme Court or by a rigid constitutional amendment on the other."[13] On April 10, he stated that he did not "agree with those who seek to amend the federal Constitution."

Two months before the election, Ford met with the leaders of the National Conference of Catholic Bishops. In writing, he assured them that he "consistently opposed the 1973 decision of the Supreme Court" and "each new life is a miracle of creation. To interfere with that creative process is a most serious act."[14] At the October 22, 1976, debate, Ford strongly endorsed the Republican platform and the constitutional amendment to outlaw abortion. Carter, by contrast, said that he opposed a constitutional amendment, but that he would do everything he could to reduce the need for abortion.

Congressman David Obey (D-WI) criticized the Catholic bishops for "appearing to be subtly blessing the candidacy of one candidate for president simply on the basis of his position on abortion" and not take into account "the candidates views on other great moral issues, such as poverty and racial justice."

The House approved the Hyde Amendment, but the Senate was not as willing to deny federal funds for abortion. Republican floor manager Senator Edward Brooke opposed the abortion amendment because it discriminated against the poor. Republican Senator Bob Packwood opposed the amendment because it was a total prohibition and "no matter how dire the medical circumstances, no matter how endangered the life of the woman, there will be no federal funds for abortion." He offered an amendment to strip the House language, which was approved by the Senate by a vote of 57 to 28. Fourteen Democrats, including Senators Biden, Ford, and Byrd, and 14 Republicans opposed the amendment.

The House insisted on their language, and Congress hit a stalemate over abortion funding.

Representative Silvio O. Conte (R) offered compromise language to provide an exemption "where the life of the mother would be endangered." The language passed the Senate with the support of 29 Democrats and 18 Republicans. Senators Byrd, Leahy, Bayh, and Kennedy were among the supporters of the amendment. Democrat Warren Magnuson urged his colleagues to pass the bill immediately and send it to the president because millions of people were depending on the money. Republican Senator Brooke once again led floor opposition and spoke against the amendment because it "discriminated against the poor."

Despite the overwhelming support for restricting federal funding of abortion, President Ford vetoed the bill on September 29, 1976. The House and Senate both overrode the president's veto[15] on September 30, 1976, and the Hyde Amendment became law (P.L. 94-439) without the president's signature.

The 1976 language was never implemented because it was challenged, and temporary restraining orders were imposed in New York by Judge John Dolling of Brooklyn and the District of Columbia.[16] On June 22, the Supreme Court ruled that states did not have to pay for abortions, and sent the New York and D.C. cases back to the states. The Congress started the battle anew in 1977.

After six months, compromise language was reached in the House and Senate to provide exceptions for rape, incest, and the life and health of the mother. However, two physicians would have to determine that the woman would "suffer severe and long-lasting physical health" problems to justify an abortion solely on health reasons. The compromise language passed the House by a vote of 201 to 155 with the support of 103 Democrats and 98 Republicans. Among the supporters were future chairman of the Ways and Means Committee Congressman Dan Rostenkowski (D-IL), future governor of Michigan Jim Blanchard, and Congressman Markey (D-MA).

President Carter, who defeated Ford in the election, preferred the 1976 language and opposed the changes which provided more exceptions. However, when it was presented to him, he signed the legislation because he opposed federal funding of abortion.

President Ford's position on abortion became much clearer after he left office and now sits on the Advisory Committee for Republicans for Choice.

Carter felt strongly against federal funding for abortion and appointed Joe Califano, who publicly opposed federal funding of abortion, to head up the Department of Health, Education and Welfare. This would prove to be an important appointment for pro-lifers trying to end federal funding of abortion. Califano, who also served as a top domestic aide to President Lyndon Johnson, would play a critical role in limiting public funding of abortion. In a Q&A session in

Clinton, Massachusetts, Carter said that he and Califano would work to make sure that federal money was not used for abortion and he wanted to work to ensure that "every child was a wanted child" through "adequate instruction, to provide birth control opportunities for those who believe in them, and also make sure that there is a government attitude to discourage abortions as much as possible."[17]

The Hyde language and the regulations were not as strong as the president requested. Califano wrote, "Over our objection, Congress enacted a law that also permitted Medicaid funding of abortions in cases of rape or incest 'promptly reported.' At that point, my choice was to enforce the law or, as some suggest, to resign. I was not about to retire to some Walden Pond or Vatican Hill. So I issued regulations giving women 60 days to report cases of rape or incest, recognizing that in those days most women did not report such horrendous incidents unless they thought they were pregnant. The Catholic hierarchy erupted. So did President Carter. Both wanted a much shorter period; the bishops because they thought it would curb abortions, Carter because he thought it would reduce the opportunity for fraud. I held firm, believing that I had fairly reflected congressional intent. The Congress agreed with me."[18]

Of the abortion issue, Califano said that "the issue is framed by the preposterous litmus test that each of the political parties has. If you want to be the national Democratic nominee you must be pro-choice; if you want to be the Republican national nominee you must be pro-life." In a recent interview, he said, "It's an issue over a four-year term that no president is likely to spend more than a few hours on.

And we have a war in Iraq, we have health care problems, we have 13 percent of our people in poverty, we have millions of people addicted to drugs, we have unemployment. So why that particular litmus test?"[19]

In an August 22, 1976, Senate floor debate, Senator Jesse Helms accused pro-choice advocates of supporting abortion because it would cost the government less money to abort the children than to bring the child into the world.[20] Dr. Louis Hellman of the Department of Heath, Education and Welfare had previously stated that forcing women to carry their children to term would cost the government "between $450 million and $565 million." Helms further stated that members should not vote against the Hyde Amendment under the auspices "that innocent human lives can and, indeed, should be subordinated to the monetary interests of the state."

Senator Packwood defended his position by stating he did not oppose the Hyde amendment for a cost benefit analysis, he opposed it because "a woman is entitled to determine for herself whether or not she wants to terminate an unwanted pregnancy." Those same arguments are used today by NARAL.

Democratic Senator Stennis stated that this was not a political issue or a legal question and wondered how the Supreme Court could lay down "guidelines." He stated that taking a life is murder and it is a question of "old-fashioned morality." He predicted that "as certain as night follows day that we are getting lost in the trace here, and it is going to result in a lot of terrible consequences." Senator Eagleton spoke in support of the Hyde Amendment and noted that presidential nominee Jimmy Carter opposed "the use of federal money for abortions."

Senator Packwood addressed the morality issue with the fact that millions of people were morally opposed to the war in Vietnam, yet it did not stop the government from spending millions of taxpayer dollars to fund the war.

U.S. Solicitor General Robert Bork on March 26 wrote a brief to the Supreme Court stating that states should be permitted to deny Medicaid funding of abortion. This brief would later come back to haunt him when he was nominated for the Supreme Court.

In 1976 and 1977, there were almost 100 bills proposed to amend the Constitution to make abortion illegal. Senator Jesse Helms asked the Senate to consider his bill to make abortion illegal. Senator Bayh, who opposed the Helms amendment, made a motion to kill the Helms proposal. He was successful and Helms did not get a vote on his measure. An equal number, 20 Democrats and 20 Republicans, opposed Senator Bayh. Senator Leahy from Vermont was one of the senators who opposed the Bayh Amendment.

A 1976 Supreme Court decision, *General Electric* v. *Gilbert*, ruled that employers did not have to cover pregnancy in their disability plans. A 1972 Equal Employment Opportunity Commission (EEOC) stated that pregnancy discrimination violated Title VII of the Civil Rights Acts of 1964. S. 955 sought to address the ruling and reaffirm the 1972 guidelines. The legislation prohibited discrimination against pregnant women, and required employers' health insurance and disability plans to cover pregnant women. When the bill came to the Senate floor, Senator Eagleton offered an amendment to prohibit coverage for abortion services unless the mother's life was endangered. Senators Biden, Stennis, and DeConcini joined Senator Eagleton in opposing the motion to kill his amendment. Their efforts failed.

In an effort to help pregnant women, Senator Kennedy and Senator Bayh introduced legislation to fund life support centers that would provide "open and unbiased counseling before the abortion is recommended and permitted."[21] There were also efforts to address day care for the working poor.

Supporters of the bill sported orange buttons that read "HR 9803: Day Care no Welfare." President Ford vetoed a bill to provide day care centers for the poor on April 6, 1976. Fifty-eight Republicans joined 243 Democrats to override the veto on May 4 by a vote of 301 to 101. The Senate was three votes shy of overriding the veto and the House and Senate went back to work and offered Ford another chance to sign childcare legislation. He signed the bill and it became P.L. 94-401.[22]

The pressure against pro-life Democrats continued to build, and the tools used to push them away from the party were becoming effective. In the 1978 election, the Democratic constituents of Congressman Mike Blouin, who supported the Hyde Amendment, decided to teach him a lesson for not changing his position on abortion. They voted for other races where pro-choice Democrats were running, but refused to back him because he was pro-life and didn't bow to the pressure to change. As a result, Congressman Blouin lost his re-election bid, and Republicans have held the seat ever since. Democrats have a chance to reclaim the seat since Congressman Nussel is not seeking re-election. Pro-life Democratic candidate Bill Gluba ran against Nussel in 2004 and is once again seeking the seat. He won 43 percent of the vote last time around and has a good chance of winning if Democrats rally behind him. Of the 1978 loss and the Democratic Party's stance on abortion, Congressman Mike Blouin, first elected to Congress in 1972, said that "pro-life Democrats didn't leave the party, they were pushed out."

In Blouin's current gubernatorial race, abortion is proving to be an issue once again. Instead of debating the issues and his strong credentials, his opponents are focusing on his pro-life position.

Pro-choice advocates lost their Republican leader in the Senate when Senator Brooks was defeated in 1978 and the Democratic Party continued to move toward a strong abortion rights position.

Endnotes

1. *New York Times*, May 28, 1976, sect. 1, p. 13.
2. Interview, MSU Vincent Voice Library.
3. Christopher Lydon, *New York Times*, February 4, 1976, p. 53, col. 1.
4. *New York Times*, February 4, 1976, p. 15, col. 1.
5. *Kennebec Journal*, Augusta, July 14, 1976.
6. *The News*, Port Arthur, Texas, March 7, 1976.
7. Interview with Jim Killilea, March 2006.
8. He would not refer to Jimmy Carter by name. He explained early in his speech that mention of Carter's name "would allow his [Carter's] supporters to spend several minutes of my time for applause and I am permitted only a few minutes to speak out."
9. *The Post Standard*, July 20, 1976.
10. Congressional Quarterly Almanac, 1976.
11. Interview with Congressman Jim Oberstar.

12. Public Papers of the Presidents, Gerald R. Ford, News Conference, Strafford Room, Memorial Union Buidling, University of New Hampshire, 67 (7).

13. Public Papers of the Presidents, Gerald R. Ford, Buffalo Grove High School, March 13, 1976, 210 (6).

14. Public Papers of the Presidents, Gerald R. Ford, Letter to the Most Reverend Joseph L. Bernardin, 770.

15. House Roll call vote #848 (312-93) and Senate Roll Call Vote #864 (67-15).

16. "Religious Groups Take Action to Block Anti-abortion Law," *Valley News*, California, October 21, 1976, p. 4, sect. 1.

17. Public Papers of the Presidents, Jimmy Carter, p. 392.

18. Joseph Califano, "The Bishops and Me: How I Squared Church and State," *The Washington Post*, June 27, 2004, p. B1.

19. Joe Feuerherd, "House Catholics Promote Dialogue, but Few Want to Talk (or Listen); Chris Smith Sees Inconsistency, Joe Califano Complexity; Who Killed JFK?" *National Catholic Reporter*, April 21, 2004.

20. Congressional Record, August 25, 1976, p. 27672.

21. Congressional Record, July 28, 1976 page 20885.

22. 1976 Congressional Almanac, p. 620.

CHAPTER 10

1980: The Gathering Storm (A Chill Wind Blows)

"I don't believe in abortion on demand. The day we can solve the world's population problem, the problem of browns in Central America, the problems of blacks in the ghetto, by aborting them, that's unacceptable to me. How about the kids in mental hospitals: they're parasites on the environment. How about the old people in the institutions: they're cluttering up the landscape. Do you want to exterminate them, too?" — Senator Ted Kennedy, 1970 Campaign for Senate

President Carter's approval rating was at a historic low; inflation was high as was the unemployment rate. The hostage crisis in Iran added to the concern about Carter's abilities as president. With Carter's re-election chances slipping, Kennedy supporters saw an opportunity. Draft Kennedy groups formed to urge him to run.

The 1980 Convention rules required delegates to vote for the presidential candidate they were elected to support for at least the first convention ballot. The delegates could only be released from the commitment if they received the declaration in writing from the candidate they were sent to support. Carter had a majority of the delegates and would win, barring any rule change. Kennedy supporters would have to fight and win the rule change if their candidate was going to have any chance of winning. Carter, on the other hand, needed every vote to prevent a rule change. His supporters vehemently opposed the resolution. If he was going to be the nominee, winning this fight was critical.

Kennedy delegates arrived at the convention hall four hours before the convention and secured the seats near the phones.[1] There was heated discussion, and when the vote occurred, delegations were split. Several large states passed on the vote the first time through roll call. The motion was defeated, but only after Kennedy withdrew his quest for the presidency. This allowed credentials chairwoman Connecticut Governor Ella Grasso to bring the credentials report to the floor free from controversy.

Kennedy spoke on Tuesday, the second night of the convention, and outshined President Carter. His popularity in the party was strong, and Carter knew it.

Senator Kennedy and a slew of special interest groups heavily contested Carter's initial platform. Carter needed to show a united party, and had to appease Kennedy supporters. Kennedy pushed the platform on abortion and other issues, claiming a tremendous victory. As a result of Kennedy's brilliant political maneuvering, eight of his minority reports were adopted right away, with another six adopted later.

Many blame Carter for the abortion takeover of the party and associate his position in sync with the pro-choice groups because it was under his reign that the abortion rights supporters had their first victory.

Gloria Steinem, New York member of the Platform Committee and spokeswoman for women's rights, founded the National Women's Political Caucus in 1971. She was also the founding editor (1972) of *Ms.* magazine. It was Steinem that made the motion to support Medicaid funding of abortion and it was approved. Despite the victory, Steinem was disappointed with Carter, and four years later she criticized him for not doing anything for women's rights and blamed him for not one state passing the ERA since he was elected. She refused to endorse him.[2] At a 1977 Women's Political Caucus meeting, Steinem warned women not to support candidates who didn't totally agree with issues including "reproductive freedom, the ERA, economic parity, children care programs, and job training." She denounced Carter for supporting the ban on Medicaid funded abortions.[3] Not everyone agreed with her position. The Missouri delegate overwhelmingly opposed abortion. Delegation Chairwoman Anne O'Donnell said, "I have always been a feminist, but I don't plan on being driven out because I oppose abortion."

Some delegates were not happy with inclusion of an abortion plank. Missouri Delegate Fran Noonan resigned as a delegate to protest the pro-choice platform plank.[4]

Yet, the theme of the convention seemed to be about how important the right to have an abortion was for women. One speaker was Boston obstetrician and gynecologist Dr. Kenneth Edelin. In 1973, he performed an abortion on a woman who was five or six months pregnant. He was later tried and convicted of manslaughter. He stated that public funding of abortion was needed and that minority and poor women deserve it.

The 1980 platform read:

> Reproductive Rights — We fully recognize the religious and ethical concerns which many Americans have about abortion. We also recognize the belief of many Americans that a woman has a right to choose whether and when to have a child.
>
> The Democratic Party supports the 1973 Supreme Court decision on abortion rights as the law of the land and opposes any constitutional amendment to restrict or overturn that decision.
>
> Furthermore, we pledge to support the right to be free of environmental and worksite hazards to reproductive health of women and men.
>
> We further pledge to work for programs to improve the health and safety of pregnancy and childbirth, including adequate prenatal care, family planning, counseling, and services with special care to the needs of the poor, the isolated, the rural, and the young.

In an August 13, 1980, letter to the platform committee, Carter wrote, "Since the beginning of my administration, I have personally opposed federal funding of abortion. I am sworn to uphold the laws passed by Congress, and the Constitution of the United States as interpreted by the Federal Courts, but my personal view remains unchanged."[5]

Kennedy, on the other hand, had a strong pro-life record until the late 1970s. Before *Roe* v. *Wade*, he stated, "Legalization of abortion on demand is not in accordance with the value which our civilization places on human life." During his 1970 campaign, Senator Kennedy spoke against using abortion as a form of population control. When Kennedy, the number one Catholic politician in the country, changed his position on abortion, other Democrats felt more comfortable in changing their position also.

In 1980, reproductive rights and the freedom to choose became the new buzzwords and the Democratic Party fully embraced "protecting women's rights" on abortion. Protecting women's rights was the right idea, but the sole focus on reproductive rights and abortion was the wrong way to achieve that goal. They should have focused on equal pay and equal job opportunities for women, childcare, child support enforcement, and other true women's issues. The leaders in the feminist movement who pushed for the focus on abortion rights failed the Democratic Party.

However, the party did not know how to handle this new idea of abortion. No one stood up to retain space for pro-life Democrats. In 1976, there were 125 pro-life Democrats in the U.S. House of Representatives. Today, there are only 30, and, as Congressman Oberstar has said many times, "They didn't stop sending people to Congress, they just stopped sending Democrats."[6]

People who would benefit from Democratic policies left the party. Conservative union men who would benefit from the Democratic Party's strong advocacy for workers' rights and safety in the workplace voted for Reagan and turned their backs on the Democratic Party. Others were alienated over cultural issues and started voting Republican. We lost a wing of the party. Many Democratic leaders changed their position on abortion in the 1980s because they listened to the loudest voices rather than the smallest. Was it a self-fulfilling spiral?

A pro-life Democratic committeewoman from Minnesota said "I am a Democrat," and "in many states there are Democratic senators in deep trouble this year because of their pro-choice record." She was proven right in 1980 when the Republicans picked up 12 new seats, defeating 9 incumbents, and Reagan defeated Carter. The Republicans had already started courting the southern voters, and Reagan laid claim to the South when he announced his candidacy for president in Mississippi.

The Democratic Party's position moved more toward abortion rights, but there was a general discomfort. Leading Democrats in the House continued to fight against Medicaid funding of abortion. Democrat Congressman William Natcher led the fight to keep the more restrictive language, approved by the House, against Medicaid funding of abortion. The more liberal Republicans in the Senate were insisting on their version.[7] The House wanted to eliminate federal funding of abortion in the cases of rape and incest.

Senator Ted Stevens (R-AK) succeeded in removing a provision to protect children and women. The amendment would have required reporting for incest and increased the reporting time for rape victims. Senator Helms tried to defeat the Stevens language but he could only get 15 Republicans and 13 Democrats to join him. Senators Lugar, Heinz, Baker, Tower, and Warner were among the Republicans who voted against the Helms Amendment. Democratic Senator Boren was among the 13 Democrats who supported Helms.

The House voted to prevent abortion funding for the Federal Employees Health Benefit Program with the support of 106 Democrats including Democratic Congressmen Shelby from Alabama, Billy Tauzin from Louisiana, and Ralph Hall from Texas, who later changed their party affiliations. Democratic Congressmen Nelson (FL), Markey (MA), Gephardt, and Al Gore also supported the amendment.

In 1981, Senator Helms introduced legislation to define all human beings as existing from the "moment of conception" and empower the states to protect them. Blackmun wrote in *Roe* v. *Wade* that if a fetus is a child, he is protected under the 14th Amendment. The overall discomfort with abortion continued to grow as did support for the Helms bill. There was a sincere interest in trying to determine when life began. Senator East, Subcommittee Chairman, called in 34 scientists with half testifying that life does, in fact, begin at conception. The other half agreed that life begins at conception but qualified their statement with "we do not know when personhood begins."

Senator Hatch was the chairman of the full committee and refused to bring the Helms bill forward because he had a different strategy. Senator Hatch introduced a constitutional amendment that would reverse *Roe* v. *Wade* and leave it up to the states to decide on abortion. Hatch had the support of the Catholic Conference and the National Right to Life Committee. At the hearing, four Catholic cardinals endorsed the legislation and put the bishops on record. When the Senate voted on the Hatch bill, it failed by a vote of 49 to 50, with Senator Helms abstaining.

The NRLC repudiated the idea of states rights and presented the Hatch strategy as a fait accompli. There was a civil war within the pro-life movement with the Catholic Conference and NRCL on one side supporting Hatch, and the conservative movement and other pro-life groups supporting Helms. Abortion was becoming more of a political issue that didn't appear to have any resolution.

Senators Biden and Goldwater changed their positions this year. Senator Biden was pro-life until 1981. Both had 100 percent pro-life voting records but were caught in the crossfire of war in the pro-life movement. If you supported one strategy but opposed another, you lost the support of one-half of the pro-life movement. They both voted against the Hatch bill. The Helms bill may very well have passed had the bill been brought before the Senate.

President Ronald Reagan spoke about the sanctity of life, but never wasted any political capital. There was a 250-seat pro-life majority, and a majority of the country sided with the pro-life position. A prime opportunity to end abortion was lost.

In Pennsylvania, Governor Casey signed the Abortion Control Act of 1982. The legislation imposed a 24-hour waiting period for women seeking abortion, required parental notification, required the woman to sign a statement that she had notified her husband she was seeking an abortion, prohibited abortion after 24 weeks in Pennsylvania, and required doctors to provide women full disclosure about the risks associated with both abortion and pregnancy and provide information about available state assistance.

By the 1982 deadline for ratification of the ERA, they were three states short, with only 35 approving the proposal. The ERA was reintroduced but stalled in the U.S. Congress.

The Supreme Court ruling in 1982 on *Akron* v. *Akron Center for Reproductive Health* struck down a requirement that second and third trimester abortions must be performed in hospitals, that parental consent must be given for minors, and that a physician must explain the development of the fetus and the risks associated with an abortion. It also struck down a requirement that fetal remains be disposed of in a humane fashion and the 24-hour waiting period. It was a major blow to pro-life advocates. The Court did uphold a Virginia law that required second and third term abortions be performed in hospitals because they allowed "outpatient surgical clinics" to be considered hospitals under that law. Justices O'Connor, White, and Rehnquist dissented. O'Connor criticized the *Roe* decision and the trimester framework set forth in the 1973 decision.

Senator Tom Eagleton (D-MO) came up with a new strategy in the 98th Congress. He introduced legislation to return the decision making to the states with respect to abortion that would return the country to the pre-*Roe* status where states determined the legality of abortion. His bill read, "A right to abortion is not secured by this Constitution." He offered his amendment to S.J.Res. 3, Hatch's bill to restrict abortion. Senator Hatch agreed to remove his language and replace it with Senator Eagleton's bill.

The strongest opponents to Eagleton's approach were the pro-life purists who wanted an all-out ban and did not agree with this approach even though it would have overturned *Roe* v. *Wade* — a goal of the pro-life community.

A recent *National Journal* poll indicated that Republicans do not want to overturn *Roe* v. *Wade* because they "would lose a good issue" and the Democrats would win because their Republican "activists would throw a party and go to sleep."[8]

Debate continued on Medicaid funding of abortion. During a September 22, 1983, floor debate on the Conte Amendment, Congressman Henry Hyde assured members that the "life of the mother" exception would be put back in conference. After the vote, Congressman Conte rose to ask that the amendment as adopted be amended to include a "life of the mother" exception. Congressman Hartnett objected to his request. Congresswoman Ferraro spoke in opposition to the amendment because it discriminated against poor women because abortions "will continue to be available to anyone who can afford them." There were 231 for and 184 against.

The Fiscal Year 1984 Labor, Health and Human Services Education Appropriations bill continued to prohibit Medicaid funding of abortion. The Conte Amendment passed the House with the support of 100 Democrats and 131 Republicans on September 22, 1983. Democratic Congressmen Gibbons (FL), Neslon (FL), Durbin (IL), Rostenkowski (IL), Markey (MA), Daschle, and Gore supported the amendment to prohibit Medicaid funding of abortion.

A majority of Democratic leaders were pro-life, yet the pro-choice voices were drowning out their voices.

Endnotes

1. *New York Times*, August 12, 1980.

2. Jura Koncius, *Washington Post*, December 20, 1979, p. C2.

3. Megan Rosenfeld, "Steinem Urges Women to Transcend Party," *Washington Post*, July 16, 1979.

4. Mike Feinsilber, "Not All Democratic Delegates Got What They Wanted," *Syracuse Herald-Journal*, August 14, 1980.

5. Congressional Almanac, 1976.

6. Interview with Congressman Jim Oberstar.

7. Congressional Quarterly Almanac, 1981.

8. James Barnes and Peter Bell, "Political Insiders Poll," *National Journal,* September 3, 2005, p. 2627.

CHAPTER 11

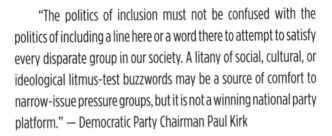

Pro-Choicers Building Influence

"The politics of inclusion must not be confused with the politics of including a line here or a word there to attempt to satisfy every disparate group in our society. A litany of social, cultural, or ideological litmus-test buzzwords may be a source of comfort to narrow-issue pressure groups, but it is not a winning national party platform." — Democratic Party Chairman Paul Kirk

The Democratic Party clearly supported the pro-choice position in 1984, yet there were still voices cautioning the party about the abortion issue further weakening the party, and there were still a large number of pro-life Democrat elected officials. It was the first convention seriously covered by C-Span and CNN, and there was an enormous amount of media competition.

At the 1984 convention, a group called Democrats For Life formed to eliminate the abortion plank in the platform. Richard Kneip, who served as the governor of South Dakota from 1971 to 1978, led the group. Kneip was the fourth

Democrat elected to serve as South Dakota's governor and at the age of 38 he was the youngest governor the state had ever elected. He and his wife, Nancy, had eight sons. Governor Kneip resigned in 1978, when President Jimmy Carter nominated him to serve as the U.S. Ambassador to Singapore. He ran an unsuccessful campaign for governor in 1986 where he lost in the Democratic primary. Sadly, he was diagnosed with cancer and died in 1987.

Kneip said that his efforts failed because the "rules virtually prevented any changes." Governor Kneip said that the platform language "amounted to rubbing the issue in the noses of the people who don't believe that the Supreme Court ruled properly." The Missouri delegation opposed the abortion plank by a 47 to 20 vote[1] and cast their votes in the presidential ballot for Senator Eagleton.[2] A 1984 *Washington Post*/ABC News poll indicated that 46 percent of Democrats supported a constitutional amendment to outlaw abortion, but only 9 percent of Democratic delegates supported outlawing abortion.

Senator Fritz Mondale and Congresswoman Geraldine Ferraro ran in 1984 and supported "a woman's right to choose." Ferraro was the first woman chosen for a national ticket by a major party. She was a respected member of the House of Representatives, where she had served for three terms. Gary Hart and Jesse Jackson also sought the nomination. Jackson was able to add five minority reports to the platform including one to strengthen affirmative action.

Ferraro justified her pro-choice position on abortion by stating that while she personally opposed abortion, she would not seek to impose her "religious views" with respect to the law.[3] Many Democrats, including Senator John Kerry in the 2004 presidential race, echoed her personally opposed reference to abortion.

Ambassador Ray Flynn spoke at the convention about the "dignity and value of human life" and accentuated his commitment to social justice.

While the Democrats continued to be courted by the pro-choice crowd, the pro-lifers closely aligned themselves with the Republican Party. At a 1984 National Right to Life Convention, they firmly stood behind President Reagan. A videotaped message from President Reagan and a video-taped message from Jerry Falwell were the highlights. Many Democrats expressed their discontent that the Democratic Party had distanced themselves from pro-life Democrats, but they weren't entirely comfortable in the Republican Party either. Rosemary Bottcher, with Feminists for Life, said, "It's hard to be pro-life and liberal. . . . Sometimes we have to hold our noses when we vote." Rita Radich, the executive director of Democrats For Life, said, "We do resent being pushed out of our party." Sandra Faucher, director of the NRLC PAC claimed that Democrats who were pro-life were denied funding by their own party. She further stated that the Democratic National Committee denied NRLC the opportunity to place an advertisement in the Democratic National Convention guidebook because they were a pro-life group.[4]

The pro-life movement turned their resources and alliances to the Republican Party and became more entrenched, while sadly, the Democratic Party moved further into an alliance with the pro-choice forces.

On September 13, 1984, pro-life Democrats had another setback when Governor Mario Cuomo delivered his famous speech, "Religious Belief and Public Morality: A Catholic Governor's Perspective," at Notre Dame. There was buzz about him seeking the presidency, and he was an influential leader in the party. *Newsweek* ran a piece about "Cuomo the Catholic." However, Archbishop John O'Connor challenged Cuomo on a local television station to defend his position on abortion. Archbishop O'Connor could not understand nor allow justification for a Catholic to, in good conscience, support abortion. Cuomo responded in his infamous speech at Notre Dame. As a Catholic, he believed that abortion was sinful, but this was a private view. He effectively rationalized that he was not obligated to work for the Catholic dogma, and the Democratic Party bought the argument.

Congressman Dick Gephardt had almost a 100 percent pro-life voting record in his early career. He voted in support of federal funding for abortion when first elected to Congress, but had a strong pro-life voting record until the mid-80s. A May-June 1985 newsletter issued by the National Pro-life Democrats Group highlighted Gephardt and his presidential aspirations. "For the first time since the Supreme Court's *Roe* v. *Wade* decision in 1973, there is a serious Democratic aspirant for the presidency with impeccable pro-life credentials and mainline support in the party."

His pro-life record declined in the mid-80s and he publicly changed his position on abortion in 1986. When he was elected to Congress in 1977, Gephardt supported a Constitutional Amendment to ban abortion.[5] His last pro-life vote was to prohibit federal funding of abortion at military facilities.

The pro-choice movement continued to build influence over the Democrats and convinced party leaders that the pro-choice position was the majority opinion of American voters and advancing the position would benefit the party.

Prior to the shift in alliances, it was acceptable to be both pro-life and Democrat or pro-choice and Republican. Respected leaders in both the House and Senate had 100 percent pro-life, 100 percent pro-choice, or mixed voting records. Even liberal groups had not yet been drawn completely into the debate. In 1986, the American Civil Liberties Union came to the aid of a pro-life group in Livonia, Michigan, on the grounds of free speech. The Pro-life Action League was engaging in a peaceful and legal protest outside an abortion clinic. Nat Hentoff writes that the ACLU, an abortion rights supporter, saw "no conflict between the constitutional right to have an abortion and to protest abortion." The case was returned to the lower court and eventually was thrown out. However, the ACLU lost its way in the protection of free speech and now advocates for abortion.

Around this time, pro-life Democrats began to feel the heat, and many changed their positions to conform to the party platform. Current sitting Senators Bill Nelson (D-FL), Dick Durbin (D-IL), and Byron Dorgan (D-ND) all had strong pro-life records. There were pro-life Democrat women, including Marilyn Lloyd (D-TN), Lindy Boggs (D-LA), and Mary Rose Oaker (D-OH). Speaker of the House Jim Wright voted pro-life. Former members and leaders in the party such as Sonny Montgomery, Les Aspin, Marty Russo, and Dan Rostenkowski, the powerful chairman of the Ways and Means Committee, also voted pro-life. Congressman David Obey and Senator Phil Gramm supported pro-life legislation.

Most of them changed their position to avoid tough primaries from pro-choice candidates who were backed by EMILY's List. The group was founded in 1985 to elect pro-choice women candidates and did not have an overall political strategy to maintain a Democratic majority. They targeted pro-life members — regardless of party — and sought to elect pro-choice candidates. They were very successful at raising money and successful in ousting pro-life Democrats. When they succeeded, in many cases a pro-life Republican would win the seat.

After Mondale lost 49 out of 50 states in the 1984 election, the Democratic Leadership Council was founded in 1985 to address the problem of losing southern Democrats. The DLC wanted to move the party toward more mainstream middle-of-the-road views, but did not address the abortion issue.

Democratic Party Chairman Paul Kirk foresaw that the party was alienating certain constituencies by catering to special interest groups. He knew this was not a winning strategy for the party.[7] Kirk served as the chairman of the Democratic Party from 1985 to 1989 and as treasurer from 1983 to 1985. He suggested that issues such as abortion and reference to the Equal Rights Amendment not be included in the 1988 Democratic platform. Then, presidential hopeful Senator Al Gore supported Paul Kirk's efforts to strip the party platform of "litmus-test buzzwords." In a written statement, Gore said the "nominee must not be forced to carry the burden of a platform of litmus-test promises that appeal only to a narrow group of special interests."[8] Walter E. Fauntroy, Jesse Jackson's representative on the platform committee, agreed with Kirk and Gore and urged the committee to keep controversial issues, such as abortion, out of the platform to provide more comfort for the leading presidential contenders. Kirk stated, "The politics of inclusion must not be confused with the politics of including a line here or a word there to attempt to satisfy every disparate group in our society. A litany of social, cultural, or ideological litmus-test buzzwords may be a source of comfort to narrow-issue pressure groups, but it is not a winning national party platform." It was the shortest platform in the last half century with only 4,500 words. Abortion was left in the platform.

Just as Kirk was promoting the elimination of the litmus test, Supreme Court nominees were swept into the abortion debate when Judge Robert Bork was nominated in 1987. Republicans, who were riding high on the major victory of Reagan, saw this opportunity to provide Democrats with a "litmus-test nightmare"[9] and portrayed a vote against Bork as a vote for abortion, gay rights, and the liberal agenda, and against religion. Reaganites were very pleased with the position they put the Democrats in with respect to the nomination, and particularly the presidential candidates who were enmeshed in the politics of the Supreme Court nominees. The 1984 and 1988 Republican platforms commended President Reagan for his pro-life judicial nominees.

However, in 1988 the party nominated Governor Michael Dukakis and Senator Lloyd Bentsen for the ticket. Senators

Paul Simon and Al Gore had also sought the nomination. Al Gore supported the Hyde Amendment and supported an amendment to define an unborn child (from the moment of conception) as a person under the Civil Rights Act. In a letter to a constituent, he stated that his "deep personal conviction" was that "abortion is wrong." Gephardt said, "Life is the division of human cells, a process that begins at conception." He further stated that he has "always been supportive of pro-life legislation. I intend to remain steadfast on this issue." Jesse Jackson, who once endorsed the Hyde Amendment, said, "It takes three to make a baby: a man and woman and the Holy Spirit. What happens to the mind of a person, and the moral fabric of nation, that accepts the aborting of the life of a baby without a pang of conscience?"[10]

After the Dukakis loss, pro-life Democrats, led by Congressman John LaFalce (D-NY), led an effort to try to open the party's policy on abortion. He wrote a letter to Chairman Ron Brown that was signed by over a third of the Democrats in the House. He had the support of over half, but some members were afraid to sign the letter because of the political ramifications.[11] The letter expressed concern that we had devolved from the Carter era of inclusion for pro-life Democrats, and the party needed to show sensitivity so people could vote their conscience. "The Democratic party is seen more and more as the party of abortion — a sure recipe for losing irretrievably a significant segment of our traditional base of support," he said. "This issue is not going to go away," he continued. "Nor is it likely that public attitudes on this issue will change significantly given the mere passage of time. We therefore think it politically wrongheaded for our party to be on record as favoring the use of taxpayer dollars to fund an alleged 'fundamental right' that is so strongly opposed in conscience by millions of Americans and by ourselves."

The members who signed the letter personally met with Chairman Ron Brown to urge a more neutral position on abortion, but it turned out to be a lost cause. The 1988 platform stated, "The fundamental right of reproductive choice should be guaranteed regardless of ability to pay."

Society was still trying to understand fetal development, abortion, and how abortion affected women. Surgeon General C. Everett Koop was charged with reporting on the emotional and psychological affects abortion has on women. After interviewing 27 experts, Koop responded that the studies "do not support the premise that abortion does or does not cause or contribute to psychological problems." Dr. Julius Fogal, a leading expert in these areas, as he was both an obstetrician-gynecologist and psychiatrist, was not consulted in the study. Before *Roe* v. *Wade*, Dr. Fogal warned that "the trauma [of abortion] may sink into the unconscious and never surface in the women's lifetime. . . . [But] a psychological price is paid. I can't say exactly what. It may be alienation, it may be pushing away from human warmth, perhaps a hardening of the maternal instinct. Something happens on the deeper levels of a woman's consciousness when she destroys a pregnancy."[12]

Studies had indicated that somewhere between 9 and 59 percent of women experience negative symptoms after abortion. Even if we took the low number, it would still mean that 90,000 women are experiencing the negative effects of abortion each year.

Public opinion on abortion continued to favor restrictions. A CBS/*New York Times* poll showed that 39 percent of respondents believed that there should be restrictions on abortion and another 12 percent supported banning abortion. Furthermore, a KRC Communications Research poll indicated that almost half of respondents, 48 percent, favored banning abortion except in the "cases of rape, incest, profound fetal deformity or if the life of the mother is threatened."

In July 1990, the Supreme Court ruled in *Webster* v. *Reproductive Services* and gave the states more authority to regulate abortion. The case energized abortion rights supporters who feared that states would work to restrict access to abortion services. NARAL Executive Director Kate Michelman used this to push pro-choice candidates and coined, "If you're out of touch with the pro-choice majority, you're out of office."[13] And, they did have some successes. James Florio won the gubernatorial race in New Jersey and Doug Wilder won in Virginia on abortion rights platforms.

At the same time, the Catholic bishops entered the political debate. They organized a campaign against abortion, pledging to spend $5 million in 5 years. They were criticized for hiring a large PR firm, Hill and Knowlton, to help them persuade people of all faiths to oppose abortion.[14] Many thought the money should be used to help the poor.

Pro-life Democrats began to face primary challenges from pro-choice candidates backed by NARAL, NOW, and EMILY's List, and pro-life challengers backed by conservative pro-life groups who believed that only a Republican majority could end abortion. Democrat Romano Mazzoli faced a challenge from pro-choice candidates Paul Bather and Jeffrey Hutter. Senator Howell Heflin, who had a strong pro-life record, faced the strongest challenge in his career from a pro-life Republican, Senator Bill Cabaniss. Pro-life Democrat Roy Dyson faced a primary challenge from pro-choice Democrat Barbara Kreamer who campaigned on her pro-choice position. Dyson did not like to be pinned down on his position but did offer that he opposed Medicaid funding of abortion except when the woman's life is endangered. NARAL held a press conference for Kreamer as a "solid supporter of abortion." Kreamer also received the support of EMILY's List, who broke with their tradition of not opposing incumbents. [15]

Pro-life Democrat Rep. Frank Annunzio opposed abortion and faced a Republican challenger. Rep. George Sanmeister of Illinois and Wayne Owens of Utah opposed abortion except for in cases of rape or incest. Additionally, pro-life Senator Jim Exon faced a challenge from Representative Hal Daub. Exon opposed abortion with the exception for rape, incest, and life of the mother, while Daub opposed abortion in all circumstances.

Pro-life Democrat Governor Rudy Perpich faced and won a Democratic primary challenge from pro-choice Democrat Mike Hatch who ran ads encouraging people to support him and elect a "pro-choice governor." Pro-life Republicans have since claimed the Minnesota's governor's mansion as Perpich was the last Democrat elected. Also facing a pro-choice Democrat in his primary, Minnesota state representative Wayne Wood was able to defeat NARAL candidate Lew Mittness.

Then Lt. Governor Zell Miller faced a challenge from the mayor of Atlanta, Andrew Young. NARAL placed a TV advertisement which highlighted Young as the "strongest abortion rights candidate." What had previously been a close race ended with Young finishing far behind Miller and losing support from women voters.[16]

Labor unions were beginning to flirt with the pro-choice movement, and in 1990 convened to discuss supporting legalized abortion and using their lobbying time and funds to support legalized abortion. They decided to remain neutral and a July 31, 1990, statement deferred "to the individual judgments of its affiliates and their members on reproductive issues." The *New York Times* article criticized this decision, saying that "Women still have no standing in Unions. . . ." Yet, the decision had the support of its members. A 1990 Wirthlin Group Poll indicated that 77 percent of respondents thought the unions should focus on other issues, but if they had to take a position, 45 percent thought the union should take the position in opposition to abortion. Fifty-two percent of union women thought the union position should be opposed to abortion.[17]

Even though organized labor had agreed to be neutral on abortion, it has not stopped the flow of money to pro-choice groups. In the past ten years, organized labor has supported EMILY's List with over $350,000 in contributions. The National Education Association has donated between $5,000 and $10,000 per election cycle. It is an interesting approach to neutrality.

The attack on pro-choice Catholics began to pick up steam when Bishop Austin Vaughn stated that Cuomo's position on abortion puts him at "serious risk of going to hell." Cardinal Joseph Bernadin cautioned that punitive acts against Catholic politicians who vote against the teaching of the church is not the most effective way to handle the situation. He wrote the church's "consistent ethic of life" and many looked to him as the voice and leader on the abortion issue.

At a March 20, 1990, speech at the Woodstock Theological Center of Georgetown University, he stated, "The Church can be most effective in the public debate on abortion through moral persuasion, not punitive measures." He further stated that the lobbying for and against abortion has been ineffective and "it is still possible to locate the majority of Americans" who oppose "abortion on demand." Neither side on the abortion debate has "moved this middle toward a viable political and civil consensus."[18] But the pro-choicers secured their control over the Democrats.

Endnotes

1. *Kennebec Journal*, July 13, 1976.

2. Interview with Mike Schwartz.

3. *Gettysburg Times,* September 13, 1984.

4. *New York Times*, "Abortion Opponents See Reagan as 'Clear-Cut' Choice," June 10, 1984.

5. *Constitution-Tribune*, February 22, 1988.

6. Nat Hentoff, "Abortion Protestors Have First Amendment Rights, Too," *Washington Post*, February 7, 1986.

7. Interview with Paul Kirk.

8. *Washington Times*, December 9, 1987.

9. Phil Gailey, "Bork: Another Litmus Test for Democratic Hopeful?" *St. Petersburg Times*, p. 3A.

10. *World*, January 17, 1988.

11. Interview with Congressman John LaFalce.

12. Colman McCarthy, "The Real Anguish of Abortions," *Washington Post*, February 7, 1989.

13. William Saletan, "There's No Pro-Choice Majority Either," *Wall Street Journal*, June 27, 1990.

14. Mark Shields, *Washington Post*, May 1, 1990.

15. Congressional Quaterly Weekly Report, August 25, 1990.

16. Mark Shields, *Washington Post*, 1990.

17. The Wirthlin Group Press Release, March 29, 1990.

18. Laura Sessions Step, "Cardinal Tempers Abortion Debate" *Washington Post*, March 21, 1990.

CHAPTER  12

Silence

"Traditionally, Democrats have been the party of the powerless and the poor. We are the party that takes care of those who cannot take care of themselves. So, it is a tragic aberration and a bitter irony that legal abortion should have found aid and comfort in our party." — Robert P. Casey, former governor of Pennsylvania.

In 1992, there was no question that the Democratic Party supported abortion. While unity and inclusion were the themes of the convention, it was not the message the party was sending to pro-life Democrats. The party leadership had made it clear that no pro-life candidate would receive the endorsement or support of the party in a presidential race. Senator Sam Nunn (D-GA), who was considering a run, sent a letter to a constituent stating that the decision to have an abortion should be left "to the informed conscience of the mother." His record spoke differently. He had previously supported the Hyde Amendment and stated that he opposed abortion.[1]

Another presidential hopeful was then Governor Bill Clinton who stated in a letter to the Arkansas Right to Life Committee in 1986, "I am opposed to abortion and to government funding of abortions. We should not spend state funds on abortions because so many people believe abortion is wrong." Yet when he announced his candidacy he proudly stated that he "trust[s] the women of America to make the right choice" on abortion.[2] Senator Bob Kerrey wrote to a constituent, "The state of Nebraska should do all it can legally to legislatively restrict abortion." He later stated that his position changed to one that supports abortion rights.

Other candidates included Senator Tom Harkin who at one time said he opposed abortion, but clarified his position in the 1992 campaign using the Ferrara mantra of "personally opposed" to abortion but his personal views "have never gotten in the way." He voted against funding of abortion in military facilities on August 8, 1978. Candidate Jerry Brown also changed his position. In 1988, he said, after working with Mother Teresa in India, "the killing of the unborn children is crazy." Senator Paul Tsongas seemed to be the only one who was consistent in his view on abortion. He had a strong pro-choice record.

The 1992 platform cited *Roe* for the first time stating, "Democrats stand behind the right of every woman to choose, consistent with *Roe* v. *Wade*." The Democrats continued to advocate for abortion rights under Clinton.

Immediately after taking office, President Clinton removed the ban on research involving fetal tissue, but stated a commitment to "prevent unintended pregnancy" through "prenatal care, childcare, and family and medical leave that will lead to healthy childbearing and support America's families." He renewed his commitment to a woman's right to choose, but also said that the nation must reduce the number of abortions. The abortion rate dropped 16.7 percent from 1990 to 1995,[3] which many attribute to support for social programs and a better economy.

The pro-life community was outraged when, on January 22, 1993, President Clinton overturned the Mexico City Policy which prohibited federal funds from being used to fund abortion overseas or to use federal funds to lobby for abortion. Additionally, he overturned the restrictions on Title X money that could not provide abortion referrals and counseling. The pro-life community was outraged with the executive orders in the first days of his presidency which provided more fuel for the anti-Democrat sentiment.

However, Clinton did try to move the party to focus on making abortion rare, and said at a 1993 Town Hall meeting, "I think there are too many [abortions] and if we want safe, legal, and rare, we have to do more preventative outreach."[4]

The Pro-life Democrats in Congress, led by Tony Hall (D-OH), challenged the pro-choice position of the party, and this time the message for inclusion in the party was heard.

A 1996 Gallup Poll found that almost three-quarters of respondents agreed that abortion should be illegal during the third trimester of pregnancy unless the life of the mother was endangered. A majority thought that parents should be notified and also that testing should be done to determine if the child could survive outside the womb at five months. A majority of religions opposed abortion. Pro-life Democrats, armed with the statistics, set a meeting with Chairman Don Fowler to discuss the platform language. They requested that conscience language be added to the platform so that pro-life Democrats felt that they were still welcomed in the party. After several drafts, pro-life Democrats and the Democratic Convention Platform Committee agreed on language.

Pro-choice activists were unhappy with this new spirit of inclusion and vehemently opposed the compromise language. Patricia Ireland testified on behalf of the National Organization for Women at an August 5, 1996, platform hearing about the party's treatment of "sex discrimination issues." She vehemently opposed the conscience language as "an escape clause" that allows "members who favor this kind of pregnancy discrimination" to participate in the party. What she failed to mention was that millions of women had abortions because they didn't think that they had any other choice. They feared for their jobs, their lives, or their reputations. There would be no support network, no financial assistance, no childcare, and no encouragement if they wanted to bring the child to term. This was the worst kind of pregnancy discrimination.

The Republicans were trying to advance their cause by displaying a big tent policy on abortion but they were having problems as well. In 1996, attempts for a floor discussion on the GOP abortion plank failed because pro-life Congressman Henry Hyde would not allow Senator Dole to insert inclusion language for pro-choice Republicans.

George H. W. Bush had to prove his allegiance to the pro-life constituency since he previously had held a pro-choice position. The Bush family charity was Planned Parenthood and Bush was a big supporter of contraception. In the 1992 campaign, First Lady Barbara Bush expressed her feelings that "abortion is a personal issue that does not belong in the platform" just prior to the Republican Convention.[5] Furthermore, a colleague, Congressman Wilbur Mills, nicknamed then Congressman Bush, "rubbers" because of his strong record in support of Planned Parenthood and focus on birth control in Congress.

Bush's position on abortion was questioned several times during his administration. At a January 24, 1990, news conference, a reporter asked about Bush's position that abortion was a "personal choice and a question of conscience." Bush responded that he was "elected to fulfill the platform."[6]

Tony Hall spoke at the 1996 convention about being pro-life and Democratic at the request of President Clinton. There was a meeting in the White House and they decided to extend a speaking invitation to Congressman Hall. George Stephanopoulos called his Washington office and the staff explained that Tony was in North Korea and it was the middle of the night. They asked if they should wake him up. Stephanopoulos said yes. Congressman Hall, who was having a difficult time, received much more respect and better treatment from his hosts after receiving a late night urgent message from the White House.

Rick Carne, Congressman Hall's chief of staff, attended the convention with Congressman Hall. He recalls that it was surreal as he stood behind the screen on the stage with Wolf Blitzer and others. He was very proud at this moment of Congressman Hall and his courage. He said they were treated quite well and there were no problems. The

Clinton camp instructed the delegates that they were to applaud, and no booing would be tolerated. Congressman Hall received nothing but support as he said:

> I'm a pro-life Democrat. I'm one of about 40 Democrats in the Congress. And many of us have felt left out by our party's position on abortion for many years. But this year is different. For the first time, the Democratic Party has included in our platform a conscience clause on this divisive issue. It says, "The Democratic Party therefore recognizes that individual members have a right to abide by their conscience on this difficult issue and are welcome participants at every level of the party." The Democratic Party is indeed the party of true inclusions. And it is the party where every American can feel welcome and at home. We Democrats believe that our government and our whole society will be judged on how we treat the least of these among us. So we renew our pledge to be a voice for the voiceless and we reaffirm our commitment to the principle that public service is not an end in itself but rather a means to serve others. With God's help, let us make the United States the compassionate and tolerant nation it was established to be.

Democrats also heard from Kate Michelman, head of the National Abortion Rights Action League, who was given a prime-time speaking spot to talk about the Democratic Party's commitment to protect a woman's right to choose, and further cemented the idea that all Democrats support abortion.

It was evident that Gore felt some remorse or at least realized that Casey had been treated poorly in 1992. Shortly after the 1992 convention, he placed a personal call to the governor to explain why the party did not allow him to speak. Then Gore was instrumental in arranging for Bob Casey Jr., the son of the late governor, and his brother Pat, who was running for a congressional seat, to present a video presentation about their father to recognize the accomplishments and leadership he had provided to the party. They did so in the afternoon when no one was watching. However, the 60-second video developed by the DNC did reference Governor Casey as a fighter for the unborn.

Regardless of the outreach, pro-life Democrats continued to feel ostracized from the party. The pro-choice groups had done a good job of pushing pro-life Democrats away from the party if they would refuse to change their position, but the pro-choice groups had an unlikely and uncoordinated partnership with conservative pro-life groups.

All major organizations, such as the AFL-CIO, the Human Rights Alliance, the National Rifle Association, and others publish congressional scorecards to let their members know how their representative is voting in Congress on the issues that are important to them.

In a letter to his pro-life colleagues, Congressman Gene Taylor (D-MS) said that he does "not write this letter with pleasure" and expressed his concern about the National Right to Life Committee's position on campaign finance reform and believed it was politically motivated. He further presented a sample of the NRLC attorney's resume that was almost entirely Republican based and included a list of involvement of Republican activities including having served as a delegate to his Republican State Convention for the past 16 years.

In 1999, a group of pro-life Democrats headed by Congressman Jim Barcia (D-MI) met with the National Right to Life Committee (NRLC) to talk about their annually published congressional scorecards, and how those scorecards hurt pro-life Democrats by including votes that were not under the purview of the organization but were supported by the Republican Party.

The meeting was meant to discuss including campaign finance reform as a pro-life issue on the scorecard and Barcia was encouraging the NRLC to work toward a compromise bill that would not divide the pro-life Democrats and Republicans. Scoring these types of very partisan, but questionable as to how they pertain to the pro-life agenda, issues left leading pro-life Democrats with a mark on their perfect records and opened the door for pro-life organizations to oppose pro-life Democrats and support pro-life Republicans who were more likely to support the conservative issues pushed by the Republican Party.

The NRLC used the campaign finance reform vote against Congressman Charlie Stenholm. In a piece of literature handed out to pro-life supporters they attacked Stenholm for his vote against campaign finance reform and praised his Republican opponent, Rudy Izzard, for supporting "legal protection for unborn children" and not "using your tax dollars to pay for abortion." They urged pro-life voters to support Izzard and insinuated that Congressman Stenholm was not a pro-life candidate.

Congressman Stenholm said of the effort, "It's difficult to understand why a pro-life organization would even enter a race between two pro-life candidates. But what makes even less sense to me is how a pro-life organization could turn its back on a member of Congress who has a 20-year, proven voting record on pro-life issues. I have to wonder how any group expects to be taken seriously, especially by pro-life Democrats, after tactics like this."

The decisions were already made before the meeting happened. It was clear that NRLC was not going to help pro-life Democrats because of its allegiance to the Republican Party. The heated meeting ended with several members storming out. One member told the NRLC that they were "shooting themselves in the foot" and hurting the pro-life movement and said "to hell with you" before storming out. Another said, "What you did to Charlie Stenholm is immoral. I don't care if you blacklist me. I am never talking to you again." He also stormed out. Another very agreeable member said, "I have talked to my constituents, and they believe that it is ethical to vote for pro-life issues and campaign finance reform." Barcia again tried to build consensus around the pro-life issue and urged the NRLC to also discuss the funding they receive from the Republican Party. Many Democrats suspected, even prior to the vote, that the NRLC was loyal to the Republican Party and only concerned about maintaining a Republican majority.

However, it became more apparent to pro-life Democrats that party mattered more than the pro-life position when the NRLC stood up to defend then Governor Bush in 1999. Bush had a record of supporting abortion in all three trimesters for any reason. PAC Director Carol Tobias said, "Governor Bush's position would eliminate about 98 percent of all abortions currently being performed, and we would certainly regard that as a pro-life position."[7] Other pro-life leaders disagreed with the decision to support Bush. Gary Bauer called Bush's position "vague." "I don't see how a compassionate conservative can be ambiguous about protecting unborn children." American Life League President Judie Brown issued a press statement that "George Bush has abdicated his right to be described as pro-life."[8]

Frustrated with NRLC's loyalty to the Republican Party, Pat Mooney founded Americans United For Life to support candidates regardless of political affiliation. He was shut down by a lawsuit from NRLC on the grounds that the name was too similar and confusing to donors.

A few years later, during debate on the bankruptcy bill, the NRLC declined to vote on an amendment offered by Senator Schumer because several Republicans expressed an interest in casting a vote against abortion clinic violence. The Schumer amendment would have not allowed those charged with violence against abortion clinics to avoid re-paying debts.

Many Republicans agreed scoring campaign finance reform was a mistake for the pro-life movement. Freshman Congressman Ronnie Shows (D-MS) organized a bi-partisan effort to oppose scoring campaign finance reform. In a letter signed by pro-life members including Republicans Tom Coburn and Zach Wamp and Democrats Jerry Costello and Gene Taylor, they urged the National Right to Life Committee not to divide them on what unites pro-lifers and stated, "People of good will may be expected to differ on how campaign laws should be written because there is no universal moral principle such as 'Thou shalt not kill' that applies to how campaigns should be conducted. It is the universal principle 'Thou shalt not kill' that unites us, and that principle, we believe, was the single issue guiding the National Right to Life Committee." They ended the letter asking the NRLC to "reverse their decision to score votes on campaign reform and similar issues unrelated to the protections of human life." The NRLC responded that they were "the experts on how the legislation will affect the pro-life movement" and "anyway a majority of the pro-life members oppose the bill." The vote for the bill would not say a member was not pro-life, it would just show that their vote would hurt the NRLC's ability to advance the pro-life cause. However, it did not prevent the NRLC from using the vote against pro-life Democrats and contributing to the decline of pro-life Democrats in office.

Al Gore ran for president in 2000. The Democratic Primary produced a short-lived challenge from Bill Bradley who declined to run before the Democratic primaries. The Republican primary was more spirited and included a wide variety of candidates, including George W. Bush, Secretary of Education Lamar Alexander, Elizabeth Dole, Steve Forbes, John McCain, and Dan Quayle. The election was one of the closest races in history and made an exciting event for many who went to bed thinking that Al Gore would be president, only to wake up the next morning to see that George Bush had won. Television stations called Florida as a win for Gore and declared him the winner, but that call was later overturned. The race was finally called on December 12, 2000, after the Supreme Court ruled to end the recount of the votes in Florida.

Gore had an 84 percent pro-life voting record in the House of Representatives from 1977 to 1984.[9] He voted in support of amending the Civil Rights Act to redefine "person" to include "unborn children from the moment of conception." Clearly, his position had changed as political aspirations grew. In his acceptance speech he said, ". . . and let there be no doubt: I will protect and defend a woman's right to choose." Gore won the popular vote that year with 50,996,116 votes to Bush's 50,456,169, but, Bush won the election with 271 electoral votes to Gore's 266.

A *Washington Post* story said, "Abortion continued to be an issue for Gore, who was asked by reporters in Venice about comments he made during his 1976 congressional race suggesting that a woman's 'freedom to live her own life' does not always outweigh the rights of a fetus."[10]

Norm Coleman was elected and served as mayor of St. Paul, as a Democrat. In 2002, he challenged former Vice-President Walter Mondale in a bid for the senate seat vacated by Paul Wellstone. (Senator Wellstone had been killed in a plane crash just before the election.) Mondale accused Senator-elect Coleman of being an "arbitrary pro-lifer." In response, Coleman invited Mondale to join him in supporting a ban on partial birth abortions and a requirement for parental notification in cases of child pregnancy (legislation that the vast majority of Minnesotans support). Mondale stumbled for an answer, likely afraid to move from the rigid ideological position dictated by supporters of abortion rights. Democrat opponents of abortion heard Mondale's views loud and clear. A vote for Mondale meant the status quo in the Senate. Coleman won the Democratic seat and the Republicans won the majority in the Senate.

Another Midwestern state that has a long tradition of Democrats opposing abortion is Missouri, where Jean Carnahan lost her race against Senator-elect Jim Talent in 2002. Historically, there is a net benefit of approximately 80,000 votes to the candidate who opposes abortion in statewide races in Missouri. Additionally, Senator Max Cleland (D-GA), a wounded Vietnam Veteran who lost three of his limbs, was defeated in a pro-military state by opponent of abortion and Republican Rep. Saxby Chambliss (R-GA).

While several candidates who unapologetically support abortion lost their Senate bids, Senate Democrats did pick up a seat in Arkansas where Senator-elect Mark Pryor essentially ducked the abortion issue. When pressed, Pryor said that while he personally opposes abortion, he believes a woman should have the right to choose in cases of rape or incest. Combined with questions about Sen. Hutchinson's "family values," this was enough for Democrats who oppose abortion to feel comfortable supporting Pryor.

When pro-life Democrat Kathleen Blanco ran for governor of Louisiana in 2003, she had a 100 percent pro-life voting record, but supported a qualified pro-life position. Her opponent, Bobby Jindal, held an absolute pro-life position. The pro-life community rallied around Jindal and accused Blanco of being pro-abortion. However, she alienated her pro-life supporters when the Democratic Party sent out literature attacking her opponent. The flyer accused Jindal of being "willing to let Louisiana women die to protect his extreme agenda even if a women's life was in danger." She did end up winning the gubernatorial race and was the first woman elected to that position in Louisiana, but her credibility in the pro-life community was greatly reduced because of the attack on Jindal's strict pro-life position. Jindal went on to win a congressional seat in the 2004 election.

Endnotes

1. *Gettysburg Times*, September 14,1990.

2. *Chronicle-Telegram*, January 22, 1992, p. A-6.

3. CDC Abortion Survelliance Report.

4. Remarks in the ABC News Nightline Town Meeting on Health Care Reform in Tampa, Florida, Public Papers of the Presidents, Bill Clinton, 1993, Office of the Federal Register, National Archives and Records Administration.

5. David Dahl, "Look Who's Discussing Abortion," *St. Petersburg Times*, August 17, 1992, 1A.

6. Public Papers of the Presidents, George Bush, 1990, Office of the Federal Register, National Archives and Records Administration.

7. "Conservative Leaders Step Up to Defend Bush's Abortion Stand," *Dallas Morning Star*, March 21, 1999.

8. "George W. Bush – Not Pro-Life," American Life League, March 18, 1998, Press Release.

9. Dave Andrusko, "National Right to Life: Al Gore's Long Journey into the Night," *National Right to Life News*, October 1, 2000.

10. *Washington Post,* February 4, 2000, p. A06.

CHAPTER 13

Two Steps Back

> "Because we believe in the privacy and equality of women, we stand proudly for a woman's right to choose, consistent with *Roe* v. *Wade*, and regardless of her ability to pay. We stand firmly against Republican efforts to undermine that right. At the same time, we strongly support family planning and adoption incentives. Abortion should be safe, legal, and rare." — 2004 Democratic Platform

The 2004 campaign kicked off in January of 2003 with all six of the Democratic presidential candidates, Vermont Governor Howard Dean, Senator John Edwards (D-SC), Representative Dick Gephardt (D-MO), Senator John Kerry (D-MA), Al Sharpton, and Senator Joseph Lieberman (D-CT), attending a dinner sponsored by NARAL and pledging their support for a women's right to choose. The other three candidates, Carol Moseley Braun, Senator Bob Graham, and General Wesley Clark did not attend. However, all nine Democratic presidential candidates proudly proclaimed their allegiance with a woman's right to choose as the foundation for human rights. It was two steps back for the party and for inclusion for pro-life Democrats. NARAL and Planned Parenthood reaffirmed their dominance over abortion policy in the Democratic Party and also reaffirmed that the abortion litmus test was still in place.

At the dinner, Senator Joseph Lieberman (D-CT) said, "The president and so many in Congress are preparing a fresh assault on the right to choose, probably the most concerted, aggressive attacks" since the *Roe* v. *Wade* decision. He further stated, "If the president, the courts, and the Republican majority in Congress undercut or overturn *Roe*, they will compromise the rights of American women. . . ."[1]

Al Sharpton tied abortion to human rights and human dignity and the importance of "women having the say-so over their own body and over how they will decide to proceed with their life."[2] Minority Leader Richard Gephardt echoed the statement saying, "The freedom to choose has never been in more peril than it is today, and it is imperative for the Democratic party to assert and reassert its leadership and to protect this vital right."[3] Governor Howard Dean connected abortion to civil rights "because the government is so impressed with itself in promoting individual freedom they can't wait to get into your bedroom and tell you how to behave."[4]

Senator John Kerry followed, stating, "What is at stake, as you heard from almost every speaker, is not just the right to choose. And never in my years in the Senate have the rights of women been at such risk, never have women been assaulted in their citizenship here at home and in their womanhood around the globe as they have been by this administration."[5]

Congressman Dennis Kucinich, who was a long-standing and loyal pro-life Democrat, attended the dinner with a new pledge to protect a woman's right to choose. He changed his position on the abortion issue shortly before announcing his candidacy. Pro-life Democrat activists, who were ready to organize the troops to support a pro-life Democrat in the presidential race, were left with little choice in the Democratic primary when Kucinich changed his position. In a meeting with Democrats For Life, he explained that he was against criminalizing abortion and the direction the Republican Party was taking the debate on the issue. He maintained that he was opposed to abortion and believed it was wrong. He has failed to cast a single pro-life vote since he changed his position.

John Kerry became the frontrunner in the race but seemed conflicted about his pro-choice position, particularly after efforts to prevent Catholics who support abortion from receiving communion. He thought he could get away with using the Cuomo compromise language adopted in 1984 saying that he believed that life begins at conception but can't impose his personal beliefs on others.

However, he faced continued criticism and pressure from the Catholic leadership. In June of 2005, Archbishop Raymond Burke of St. Louis told Catholics that those "who vote for political candidates supportive of abortion rights have committed a grave sin in the eyes of the church, and should confess and do penance before receiving communion."[6] In his statement, Archbishop Burke enforced that "abortion trumps any other issue" when choosing who to vote for in the upcoming election.

Since Cuomo gave his speech in 1984, the Catholic Church had not necessarily accepted Cuomo's claims, but did not reject the "personally opposed" statement used so often by Catholic Democrats supporting abortion because of the strong leadership from Democrats on social justice issues. Even one of their own was able to vocally support abortion in the U.S. House in the 1970s.

Representative Robert Drinan, a Jesuit priest and a lawyer, was elected to serve in the House of Representatives in 1971. He was pro-choice and always wore his Roman collar while voting, even when voting for abortion funding.[7] He wasn't supposed to be in Congress because he never received permission from the church, but times had changed and this personally opposed exception was becoming a problem.

Kerry was caught in the middle. Democrats For Life encouraged him to adopt a more centrist position on abortion and he responded that he encouraged DFLA to keep bringing this issue up because it was important that we have a dialogue on the abortion issue. It was, in fact, an issue that the party needed to discuss.

On October 13, 2004, at the third presidential debate in Tempe, Arizona, Kerry was asked about the recent statements by Archbishop Burke that "it would be a sin to vote for a candidate like you because you support a woman's right to choose an abortion." He answered:

> I completely respect their views. I am a Catholic. And I grew up learning how to respect those views. But I disagree with them, as do many. I can't legislate or transfer to another American citizen my article of

faith. What is an article of faith for me is not something that I can legislate on somebody who doesn't share that article of faith. I believe that choice is a woman's choice. It's between a woman, God, and her doctor. That's why I support that. I will not allow somebody to come in and change *Roe* v. *Wade*.

Pro-life Democrats saw their prospect for inclusion disappear. The conscience language that Congressman Hall and the others worked so hard to include was eliminated. The 2000 language stated:

> The Democratic Party stands behind the right of every woman to choose, consistent with *Roe* v. *Wade*, and regardless of ability to pay. We believe it is a fundamental constitutional liberty that individual Americans — not government — can best take responsibility for making the most difficult and intensely personal decisions regarding reproduction. This year's Supreme Court rulings show to us all that eliminating a woman's right to choose is only one justice away. That's why the stakes in this election are as high as ever.
>
> Our goal is to make abortion less necessary and more rare, not more difficult and more dangerous. We support contraceptive research, family planning, comprehensive family life education, and policies that support healthy childbearing. The abortion rate is dropping. Now we must continue to support efforts to reduce unintended pregnancies, and we call on

all Americans to take personal responsibility to meet this important goal.

The Democratic Party is a party of inclusion. We respect the individual conscience of each American on this difficult issue, and we welcome all our members to participate at every level of our party. This is why we are proud to put into our platform the very words which Republicans refused to let Bob Dole put into their 1996 platform and which they refused to even consider putting in their platform in 2000: "While the party remains steadfast in its commitment to advancing its historic principles and ideals, we also recognize that members of our party have deeply held and sometimes differing views on issues of personal conscience like abortion and capital punishment. We view this diversity of views as a source of strength, not as a sign of weakness, and we welcome into our ranks all Americans who may hold differing positions on these and other issues. Recognizing that tolerance is a virtue, we are committed to resolving our differences in a spirit of civility, hope, and mutual respect."

By contrast, the 2004 language was reduced to a paragraph:

Because we believe in the privacy and equality of women, we stand proudly for a woman's right to choose, consistent with *Roe* v. *Wade*, and regardless of her ability to pay. We stand firmly against Republican efforts to undermine that right. At the same time, we strongly support family planning and adoption incentives. Abortion should be safe, legal, and rare.

Perhaps it was a failure by pro-life Democrats, who had faith that the party would continue to build acceptance for pro-life Democrats. Pro-life Democrats had either become complacent or felt it was a lost cause, but once again, the loudest voices were heard, not necessarily the majority voice.

It certainly did send another wake up call. Prior to 2004, Congressman Oberstar and other pro-life Democrats had constituents approach them and whisper, "I am a pro-life Democrat, too. Keep up the good work." In 2004, the silent majority started to feel a little more comfortable talking about their pro-life position, and Jim Killilea's hope that the election would show the party that they took the wrong position on the abortion issue was about to occur.

At the 2004 Democratic Convention, the pro-life message may not have been heard loudly inside the Fleet Center, but the message was heard in a 3 Steps rally held at Faneuil Hall. Founded in 1742, it was here that Sam Adams spoke so passionately on behalf of those who had no rights in the fight for fair taxation, and Frederick Douglass and William Lloyd Garrison spoke passionately about ending slavery, and it is where Lucy Stone spoke about the importance of equal rights for women.

At the 3 Steps rally, Democrats For Life called for support for protecting life, strengthening the "big tent" of the Democratic Party, and rebuilding the Democratic majority. The goal was to encourage pro-life Democrats to come home to the party and to express their support for inclusion for those who hold a pro-life position.

A lot of Democrats have been afraid to speak out on their pro-life position because they thought they were alone. An April 2004 Zogby Poll found that 43 percent of Democrats believe that abortion destroys a human life and is manslaughter, and the pro-life Democrats sported buttons that read "43 percent can't be wrong."

At the rally, ambassador to the Vatican and Mayor of Boston Ray Flynn encouraged the crowd. "Sam Adams had less people with him than we have here today. Let this be a revolution for life."

Other leading pro-life Democrats and candidates spoke passionately about protecting the rights of the unborn and about respectful inclusion for pro-life Democrats in the party. Senator Ben Nelson said, "We're here in Boston to be heard and to be represented." Congressman Charlie Stenholm and Pastor Clenard Childress energized the crowd with encouragement for a pro-life position.

Congressional candidate Silvia Delamar told the crowd that she did have a choice and she made it when she decided to lie down and she became pregnant as a result. Silvia was 16 years old and could have easily chosen an abortion. However, she chose life and graduated from high school with honors. She supported her son by working three jobs and went on to graduate from college with a political science degree. Married with two children, Silvia is working on a program, Another Chance, to help unwed mothers obtain their diploma or GED. While she lost in 2004, she is now running for a Georgia state senate seat.

The previous evening, pro-life Democrats joined together in the Massachusetts State House to celebrate a new direction for pro-life Democrats. Then Speaker of the House Thomas Finneran, a pro-life Democrat, addressed the crowd. Ambassador Flynn told the crowd, "Democrats want to win elections. It is up to us to convince them that they can win elections and be pro-life." The highlight of the evening was two heroes in the pro-life Democrat movement, Bob Casey Jr. and Eunice Kennedy Shriver.

Kevin Gluba, a pro-life Democrat from Iowa, attended his first Democratic convention to support his dad's candidacy for Iowa's first congressional seat. He was surprised that a majority of the people whom he met at the convention, whether they were pro-life or pro-choice, agreed that Democrats needed to stick together. He wrote that it was the first time that he "no longer felt like a Republican in sheep's clothing, or whatever negative label that is placed on a pro-life Democrat" and he "finally just felt like a Democrat."

Inside the convention hall, there was one sentence issued by a pro-life Democrat during his introduction of Ron Reagan, who would be talking in support of stem cell research. Congressman Jim Langevin from Rhode Island said that he respected "the sanctity of life at all stages." There were a few seconds of silence from inside the Fleet Center, then the crowd clapped politely and almost enthusiastically while they were trying to comprehend what had been said. While a majority of the pro-life community was opposed to embryonic stem cell research and it was not ideal that Congressman Langevin's support for life was spoken right before Reagan's call for embryonic stem cell research, at least he wasn't censured as Casey had been in 1992. Since his speech, several prominent pro-life Republicans have come out in support of embryonic stem cell research, including Majority Leader Bill Frist.

Regardless of the efforts to include pro-life Democrats, it had not yet reached a wide enough circle in 2004. Republicans had done a great job of labeling the Democratic Party as the party of abortion on demand, and the pro-choice groups did everything to enhance that image, not knowing that it was hurting the Democratic Party. A continued partnership will lead to a continued decline and deterioration of the Democratic Party.

The pro-choice stand on partial-birth abortion proved to be a major detriment in the election and the Democratic Party. A majority of polls showed that seven out of ten Americans believed that partial-birth abortion should be illegal. Over 30 states enacted partial-birth abortion laws banning the procedure. Ron Fitzimmons, executive director of the National Coalition of Abortion Providers estimated that 5,000 to 6,000 of these types of abortions were performed each year (much higher than the 500 to 600 previously claimed by pro-choice groups).

A 1995 study released by the National Abortion Federation said that a majority of the second and third trimester abortions were elective and for other reasons than the mother's health. In defining the partial-birth procedure, they stated that the babies die when the mother is given the anesthesia. But the gruesome pictures and description of babies being dismembered and the testimony of nurses and doctors who performed the procedure certainly didn't help the Democratic

Party. Sixty-five Democrats in the House[8] and 16 Democrats in the Senate[9] voted to outlaw the partial-birth procedure. When a key Democratic senator tried to find some common ground on the late-term abortion bill, he found that there was no interest in compromise. He tried to narrow the definition of health so it was not seen as a loophole, but it would pass the constitutional muster.

President Clinton had vetoed the bill three times and Ambassador Flynn cautioned him that the Democrats' stance on the issue was hurting the party. He said, "Banning PBA is good politics and good policy," and told President Clinton that he did not have the right people advising him on this issue.

Bush received an absolute majority over Kerry in 2004 with 51 percent of the vote.[10] Democrats attributed Kerry's loss to several things: Bush's success with 9-11, his ability to turn out faith and values voters, and Kerry's shortcomings as a candidate. He wasn't able to generate the electricity that Clinton had a decade earlier or connect with the working class. He also said in his acceptance speech, "I don't wear faith on my sleeve." Why was he afraid?

The Senate Democrats lost five key seats — South Dakota, South Carolina, North Carolina, Florida, and Georgia. Additionally, Louisiana Democrats suffered a major defeat when Rep. Vitter won enough of the votes to avoid a run-off. It was largely expected that Vitter would face pro-life Democrat Congressman Chris John in a November runoff. Instead, Vitter was able to secure over 50 percent of the vote and avoid a runoff largely due to the anti-Democratic sentiment from Catholic voters. John attended Catholic school for 12 years and had a 100 percent pro-life voting record. Yet his own parish priest told his congregation that the party matters.

Senator Tom Daschle experienced a similar fate. His voting record was quite clear that he had concerns about abortion and did not believe that it should be legal in all circumstances. He supported and voted for the Partial-Birth Abortion Ban Act in the Senate and also supported and voted for the Unborn Victims of Violence Act. His pro-life record was not strong, but his record was clear that he opposed late-term abortion and also saw the need to protect the unborn children in the womb from violence. Senator Daschle had a strong labor record and pushed for health care reforms so the uninsured could have access to health care. Yet when campaign workers went door to door, unemployed workers who had lost their jobs to cheaper labor overseas didn't want to talk about anything but abortion and gay rights. The Republican opposition succeeded in tying Senator Daschle to the Party's strong abortion rights stance. This, in conjunction with the Catholic Church's advocacy to support only 100 percent pro-life candidates, helped shape the campaign message to unseat Senator Daschle. The message sent was that Senator Daschle was a Democrat and all Democrats supported abortion on demand.

The 2004 election further deteriorated the Democrats' hold in many areas of the country. In South Carolina, pro-life Republican Congressman DeMint defeated Inez Tenebaum. Tenebaum, who was endorsed by EMILY's list, lost the seat held by Senator John Edwards. It was the first time since Reconstruction that Republicans held both

South Carolina Senate seats. John Edwards's seat went to Republican Congressman Richard Burr who defeated Clinton White House Chief of Staff Erskine Bowles. Housing and Urban Development Secretary Mel Martinez won former presidential candidate Bob Graham's seat. His opponent, Betty Castor, collected over $58,000 from EMILY's List. Congressman Isakson defeated another EMILY's list candidate, Denise Majette, in the race for the seat of retiring Senator Zell Miller.

Pro-life Democrats faced many challenges. In 2004, Joy Hearn ran for a local county property appraiser's position in Florida. Democrat Party leaders prevented her from speaking at a local Democratic Party meeting because she had a "Choose Life" license plate on her car. She was told that the party would only raise money for her and support her if she removed the license plate.

The Republicans highlighted their pro-choice leaders at their convention. Governors Arnold Schwarzenegger and George Pataki and Mayor Rudy Giuliani all spoke during prime time. Neither the media nor the Democratic Party gave the pro-choice Republican candidates who were Catholic scrutiny about how their pro-choice position conflicted with their Catholicism. The Republicans have historically not had a shortage of candidates who distanced themselves from the Republican strong pro-life plank, yet somehow it didn't seem to be a problem in the Republican Party. The chairman of the Republican Party referred to their party as the big tent party and a Google search on "big tent" in 2004 would have brought up many stories about the Republicans.

There was some good news on the pro-life Democrat front when Charlie Melancan won the Louisiana runoff in November and Ben Chandler won the special election in Georgia. The party fully supported their races.

Endnotes

1. Joseph Lieberman, transcript, speech at NARAL Pro-choice America dinner, January 21, 2003.

2. Al Sharpton, transcript, speech at NARAL Pro-choice America dinner, January 21, 2003.

3. Dick Gephardt, transcript, speech at NARAL Pro-choice America dinner, January 21, 2003.

4. Howard Dean, transcript, speech at NARAL Pro-choice America dinner, January 21, 2003.

5. John Kerry, transcript, speech at NARAL Pro-choice America dinner, January 21, 2003.

6. J. Mannies and Tim Townsend, "Burke: Voting for Abortion Rights Candidate Is a Sin," *St. Louis Post-Dispatch*, June 26, 2004.

7. Mary Meehan, "Democrats For Life," *The Human Life Review* (Summer 2003).

8. See Cong. Rec. H5373 (daily ed. July 25, 2002) (House Vote on H.R. 4695, the Partial-Birth Abortion Ban Act).

9. See Cong. Rec. S12948 (daily ed. Oct. 21, 2003) (Senate Vote on S. 3, the Partial-Birth Abortion Ban Act).

10. 2004 Congressional Quarterly Almanac, Congressional Quarterly, Inc., 2005.

CHAPTER 14

Full Circle —
Casey for Senate

> "I have long believed that we ought to make a home for pro-life Democrats. The Democrats that have stuck with us, who are pro-life, through their long period of conviction, are people who are the kind of pro-life people that we ought to have deep respect for."
> — Governor Howard Dean, *Meet the Press*, December 12, 2005

Where is the party today? Following the election, the DNC Chairman, Terry McAuliffe, announced that he would be stepping down and the race for a new party chairman began. The contenders were all pro-choice except Congressman Tim Roemer, who was urged to enter the race by the Minority Leader of the Senate, Harry Reid, and the Minority Leader in the House, Nancy Pelosi. Both later said that they had not endorsed Roemer, but merely encouraged him to enter the race.

Congressman Roemer believes that the Democratic Party has come a long way since 1992 when Casey was prevented from speaking. However, it was a tough race for him because of the new phenomena of bloggers and interest groups, which

161

combined to paint Roemer as a single-issue candidate. It made it difficult to talk about national security, education, jobs, or protecting the environment when he was painted as a pro-life candidate.

When Congressman Roemer spoke around the country, the Democratic Committee members were impressed with his poise and leadership. While he was speaking, they thought he would be a great chairman to lead the party. As soon as he stepped off the stage, the whispers would begin. Yes, he would be a great leader for the party. He co-chaired the 9-11 Commission and had extensive knowledge on national security, but he was pro-life. When Democrats listened to Roemer, they agreed as he spoke about the need to decrease not only the overall abortion rate, but also the teen abortion rate in our country, one of the highest in the industrialized world.

The pressure and threats to oppose Roemer were fierce. In a call to the chairman of a Midwestern state, the committee member revealed that NARAL had called him three or four times and threatened that they would not give any money and support for his state party if he supported Roemer in the race.

Congressman Roemer does believe some good came out of the campaign because he received encouragement from African American, Hispanic, and other voters who shared their opposition to the Democratic Party's stance on abortion and wanted to see more appeal in the party for those who are opposed to abortion.

An African American congressman from the South shared with Roemer his concern that the party was in a lot more trouble than they think on the abortion issue. The Republicans have a long-term strategy to entice pro-life voters to support Republicans, and the Democrats did not have a strategy to reach pro-life voters. However, the 2004 election may have had some effect. At the same time, the Republican Party was going into black churches, talking about abortion and gay rights, and urging parishioners to join the Republicans in their fight on these moral issues — a tactic that proved effective in 2004.

In February of 2005, Congresswoman Pelosi appointed South Carolina Congressman Jim Clyburn to head a Faith Working Group to reach out to "faith communities on common values such as fighting poverty, improving schools, speaking out against materialism and greed, providing better housing, and fighting for social and economic justice."[1] In response to this new position, Clyburn stated, "The Democratic agenda is deeply rooted in faith, but we have been less effective than we could be in communicating how our moral values guide our policies." At the 2005 Democrat Issues Conference, Congressman Clyburn led discussion on faith and values.

A May 2005 Democracy Corps report issued by James Carville, Stanley Greenberg, and Bob Shrum indicated a strategy for reclaiming the Catholic vote. President Clinton had won the Catholic vote by 7 points and Kerry had lost the Catholic vote by 13 points, a 20 percent drop for Democrats among Catholic voters — a likely ally of the Democratic Party because of their strong support for social justice. They attributed the loss to several factors, including that Catholic voters tend to vote more pro-life. They further stated that a pro-life Democrat receives a 24-point advantage and a pro-choice candidate loses 12 points among Catholic voters.

Ambassador Flynn became president of the Catholic Alliance in 1999 to increase Catholics' participation and influence in the political system. Finding and supporting candidates who are "pro-life, pro-family, pro-needy, and pro-immigrant" would be their goal.[2] He believes that Catholics need to become more politically engaged and fight for the social justice teachings of the church and the pro-life position, because their views are not being represented. When Flynn traveled with the pope, the crowds would go wild when the pope mentioned the sanctity of life. Each time he said "pro-life" he would receive a standing ovation — particularly among the young crowds. Flynn believes that we need to pay tribute to pro-life Democrats in Congress, as they are the most consistent voices in supporting the historic principles of the Democratic Party. Napoleon said he would have won the war if he had enough medals. We don't have enough medals.

In the 2005 Virginia gubernatorial race, Democrat Tim Kaine proved that Democrats could send a different message and win. He responded to Republican attacks on opposition to the death penalty. His opponent placed an advertisement to attack Kaine's position which avowed that Kaine would not have executed Adolph Hitler. Kaine responded that he opposed the death penalty, would not apologize for his views, and would uphold the law if elected governor. He was not afraid to stand up for his Catholic values and his opposition to abortion and the death penalty. He won in a red state. President Bush's press secretary Scott McClellan tried to explain away this victory for Democrats, saying that Kaine was not a "real Democrat."[3]

The chairman of the DNC, Howard Dean, continues to speak of inclusion for pro-life Democrats, and the party is supporting pro-life candidates. Pro-life Democrat Harry Reid (D-NV) is the Senate minority leader, and the top races in the country include pro-life Democrats who are supported by the party.

Democrats have an opportunity to unseat an incumbent senator in Pennsylvania. An early leader on the list of potential candidates was Governor Casey's son and namesake, Bob Casey Jr. Another candidate was Governor Casey's Republican opponent, Barbara Hafner, who two months prior to her pronouncement that she would enter the Democratic Primary changed her affiliation to Democrat. NARAL had already sent several staff members to work on her campaign. However, Democrats saw that Casey, and no other candidate, would be able to unseat Senator Santorum. Casey was the best person for the job.

Senator Chuck Schumer (D-NY), a strong pro-choice advocate and head of the Democratic Senatorial Campaign Committee, could have stayed out of the fray with regard to the primary. Instead, he led the charge to clear the field so the younger Casey could run for the seat unchallenged by another Democrat — all the focus and united Democratic effort could be on defeating Santorum. Short-lived speculation that former NARAL President Kate Michelman would enter the race ended rather quickly when she announced that she would not seek the seat. Her withdrawal almost sounded like an endorsement of Casey.

Unfortunately, the National Organization for Women could not look past his pro-life stance and endorsed a little-known candidate whose only effect would be to pull votes away from Casey. Democratic strategist Paul Begala said of a Casey victory, "Mr. Casey's rise would signal that opposition to abortion rights was not like opposition to civil rights."[4] The stance by NOW to oppose Casey should send a strong message to the Democratic leadership that abortion rights groups do not always have the party's best interests in mind. Legalized abortion matters more than party.

Endnotes

1. Press release: "Pelosi Names James E. Clyburn to Lead Faith Working Group," February 4, 2005.

2. Kevin Eckstrom, "Political Clout for Catholics — Former Envoy Hopes to Unify Faith's Divided Factions," *The Post Standard*, October 16, 1999, p. B-2.

3. Marsha Mercer, "The President of Mayberry," *Gettysburg Times*, November 15, 2005, p. A4.

4. Robin Toner, "Senate Campaign Tests Democrats' Abortion Tack," *Amherst Times*, April 23, 2006.

CHAPTER 15

Bringing Back the Party: Building a Culture of Life

"If we abandon the principle of respect for human life by making the value of a life depend on whether someone else thinks that life is worthy or wanted, we will become one sort of people.

"But there is a better way.

"We can choose to reaffirm our respect for human life. We can choose to extend once again the mantle of protection to all members of the human family, including the unborn. We can choose to provide effective care of mothers and children.

"And if we make these choices, America will experience a new birth of freedom, bringing with it a renewed spirit of community."
— A New American Compact: Caring about Women, Caring for the Unborn[1]

If there is anything we should all learn after 40 years of debating the legality of abortion, it is that we need to call a cease-fire. The abortion issue has become a game of political ping-pong to win elections. The losers are the women and their unborn children. People on all sides of this issue need to look past partisan politics to help women, unborn children, and families, so no one will suffer from abortion.

As long as the abortion rate is high and Democrats advocate for abortion on demand, it will continue to play a role in the deterioration of the Democratic Party. James Carville and Paul Begala, in *Take It Back*,[2] asked the question, why is the Democratic Party representing the fringe on this issue? A May 2005 Gallup Poll found that 22 percent of respondents oppose abortion and believe it should be illegal in all circumstances. In that same poll, 53 percent of respondents believe that abortion should only be legal in certain circumstances, with a majority supporting abortion only in the cases of rape, incest, and if the mother's life is endangered.

They also write that "Democrats routinely say they're not pro-abortion, they're pro-choice," and encourage Democrats to talk about abortion differently. But I urge Democrats to go a step further — don't talk about it, act on it. If you are pro-choice, fight for true choices for pregnant women.

Democrats should look to their own platform and history of the party for guidance. The platform says abortion should be rare. We must make every effort to follow through on helping women and families to truly make abortion a rare occurrence. Opportunity for everyone, not abortion on demand, is the core value of the Democratic Party. Democrats should not be afraid to stand up for faith, values, the poor, and the disenfranchised.

We need to send a strong message that we do not support abortion on demand and that our position on abortion will no longer be dictated by special interest groups such as

NARAL, NOW, and Planned Parenthood, who have clearly taken a position to fight for abortion.

We need to stop alienating members of our own party simply because of their view on abortion. The Democratic Party is the big tent party. Reclaim that title! The party needs to publicly embrace and welcome pro-life Democrats back into the party and promote and support alternatives to abortion. Democrats, regardless of their position on abortion, want to win elections and take back the majority so we can work toward helping Americans achieve the American dream. Continuing to push pro-life Democrats away from the party will only ensure continued Republican dominance.

The Democratic Party ought to be willing to embrace people of differing views or who have different approaches to solving the abortion issue and lead the effort to find common ground by fully endorsing the 95-10 Initiative developed by Democrats For Life of America.

Frustrated with the 2004 election and the continued criticism about the party's support of abortion on demand, Democrats For Life compiled a list of ideas about ways we could help women who are faced with unplanned pregnancy, and developed a comprehensive package to address the needs of pregnant women.

The 95-10 legislation would invest millions in a comprehensive plan that would reduce the number of abortions by 95 percent in the next ten years by promoting abstinence, personal responsibility, adoptions, and support for women who are facing crisis pregnancies. Abortion should not be the only option available to women.

American women and their families deserve better than being faced with abortion and having no solutions in place. Republicans should unite in the good faith effort to decrease the abortion rate by helping women and their families. Stop cutting programs that hurt the working men and women in this country. A majority of Americans work hourly jobs and don't have the luxury of part-time work, flex time, and maternity leave. Work with those who want to provide a better environment and a better opportunity for women to carry their children to term. Pro-life Republicans should no longer look to the Democratic Party as the enemy, and start forging relationships with Democrats who share a common goal to end abortion or greatly reduce the numbers.

The National Organization for Women website states that reproductive rights are "issues of life and death for women, not mere matters of choice."[3] Women's groups such as NOW should focus more on equal rights for women through addressing the glass ceiling, advocating for better childcare, ending discrimination in hiring practices, and the challenges women face when trying to decide between career and family, balancing career and family, or the challenges of being a stay-at-home mom. Access to abortion hasn't solved any of these issues.

Women are a majority of the population, and NOW could do so much more for women by focusing on true empowerment and true choice rather than pretending that abortion is easy and advocating that abortion is the means to achieve true equality in the workplace.

Today, there is almost hostility toward motherhood when society talks about empowerment for women, and the message sent is that having a child will hold you back and bring you down. The pro-choice groups have convinced women that an abortion or the option to have an abortion will free you and make you strong and successful. People criticized Supreme Court Justice Sandra Day O'Connor for holding back her career to care for her family, yet she was the first woman Supreme Court justice. The Minority Leader of the House of Representatives, Nancy Pelosi, is the mother of five children. If the Democrats take back the House, she could be the first woman speaker. Motherhood is an admirable and tough career. We need to support mothers who can afford to stay home and take care of their children and do more for women who would like to stay home.

Men need to stand up to the challenge and responsibility of parenthood, and stop pressuring or encouraging women to have abortions. Men and women across this country should be outraged by the recent case *Roe* v. *Wade for Men*, filed by the National Center for Men, which ultimately will only hurt children. The plaintiff argues that he did not want the child, is entitled to the same reproductive freedom that women achieved, and should not be forced to pay for the child. Financial concerns, fear of raising a child alone, and fear that a child will interfere with their school or job plans are among the reasons women seek abortions. A *Roe* v. *Wade for Men* will not help the abortion rate nor the women faced with unplanned pregnancies.

The reality is that *Roe* v. *Wade* has failed women. The fight will continue unless we address the reasons women seek abortions. The truth is, abortion is neither a peaceful nor positive solution to an unplanned pregnancy, for the mother or the child. Mohandas Gandhi, who advocated peaceful civil disobedience as a form of protest, thought abortion was violent and wrote, "It seems to me clear as daylight that abortion would be a crime."[4] More evidence has been collected that abortion causes many negative results for women.

There are some women who claim that abortion has not hurt them and they haven't experienced any negative side effects. Author Patricia Lunneborg claimed that a majority of 100 post-abortion women she interviewed found abortion to be a positive experience and provided them with a sense of relief.[5] However, groups such as Silent No More and Operation Outcry tell the stories of women who regretted having the abortion — even 20 or 30 years later — which prove otherwise.

We need to understand why women seek abortion and accept the results. Abortion is not empowering for most women who pay the price in the form of eating disorders, higher rates of depression and suicide, regret, and higher chance of breast cancer and other mental and physiological effects.[6] Dismissing an abortion-breast cancer link or denying the emotional and physiological problems haunting those who had abortions will do little to help the situation.

Abortion is being used as a way to solve a problem that society should be solving. I look forward to the day when both Democrats and Republicans are supporting policies to greatly reduce the number of unwanted pregnancies and abortions. Whether you are a Democrat, Republican, pro-choice, or pro-life, we all have a responsibility to be on the front lines of helping pregnant women bring their children to term.

The Democratic Party is the big tent. The other day, I had a meeting at the Democratic National Committee. While waiting for my meeting to begin, I felt like a celebrity as a string of DNC staffers came in to welcome and encourage me in the work we are doing. A new partnership is developing. However, across the country, pro-life Democrats are still trying to participate in the Democratic Party, and pro-choice advocates are still telling them that they cannot. Our journey is far from over as we carry on this torch for inclusion in the party for the silent majority. I am reminded of the words first spoken by William Lloyd Garrison when faced with a party and a Supreme Court that supported slavery, and repeated by Jim Killilea at the 1976 Democratic Convention:

> I am in earnest — I will not equivocate — I will not excuse — I will not retreat a single inch — and I will be heard.

In closing, to all those who are serious about reducing or eliminating abortion, let us go forth and work together. In the 1992 New York Times advertisement where Governor Casey and others called for a New American Compact, they said:

> In sum, we can and we must adopt solutions that reflect the dignity and worth of every human being and embody understanding of the community's shared responsibility for creating policies that are truly pro-women and pro-child. What we seek are communities and policies that help women to deal with crisis pregnancies by eliminating the crisis, not the child.

Endnotes

1. Advertisement in the *New York Times* during the 1992 Democratic Convention. It was signed by Governor Bob Casey, Eunice and Sargent Shriver, Nat Hentoff, and other leaders in the pro-life movement.

2. James Carville and Paul Begala *Take It Back: Our Party, Our Country, Our Future* (New York: Simon & Schuster, 2006).

3. National Organization for Women website.

4. Mohandas Gandhi, *All Men Are Brothers, Autobiographical Reflections* (New York: Continuum, 1980), p. 150.

5. Patricia Lunneborg, *Abortion: A Positive Decision* (New York: Bergin & Garvety 1992),

6. "Reversing the Gender Gap," The Elliot Institute, 2004.

Attachment 1	
Political Party Platform Positions on Abortion	
Democrat	**Republican**

1976

We fully recognize the religious and ethical nature of the concerns which many Americans have on the subject of abortion. We feel, however, that it is undesirable to attempt to amend the U.S. Constitution to overturn the Supreme Court decision in this area.

The question of abortion is one of the most difficult and controversial of our time. It is undoubtedly a moral and personal issue but it also involves complex questions relating to medical science and criminal justice. There are those in our party who favor complete support for the Supreme Court decision which permits abortion on demand. There are others who share sincere convictions that the Supreme Court's decision must be changed by a constitutional amendment prohibiting all abortions. Others have yet to take a position, or they have assumed a stance somewhere in between polar positions.

We protest the Supreme Court's intrusion into the family structure through its denial of the parents' obligation and right to guide their minor children. The Republican Party favors a continuance of the public dialogue on abortion and supports the

Democrat	Republican
	efforts of those who seek enactment of a constitutional amendment to restore protection of the right to life for unborn children.
1980 Reproductive Rights — We fully recognize the religious and ethical concerns which many Americans have about abortion. We also recognize the belief of many Americans that a woman has a right to choose whether and when to have a child. The Democratic Party supports the 1973 Supreme Court decision on abortion rights as the law of the land and opposes any constitutional amendment to restrict or overturn that decision. Furthermore, we pledge to support the right to be free of environmental and worksite hazards to reproductive health of women and men. We further pledge to work for programs to improve the health and safety of pregnancy and childbirth, including adequate prenatal care, family planning, counseling, and services with special care to the needs of the poor, the isolated, the rural, and the young.	There can be no doubt that the question of abortion, despite the complex nature of its various issues, is ultimately concerned with equality of rights under the law. While we recognize differing views on this question among Americans in general — and in our own party — we affirm our support of a constitutional amendment to restore protection of the right to life for unborn children. We also support the congressional efforts to restrict the use of taxpayers' dollars for abortion. We protest the Supreme Court's intrusion into the family structure through its denial of the parent's obligation and right to guide their minor children.

Democrat	Republican
1984	
There can be little doubt that a Supreme Court chosen by Ronald Reagan would radically restrict constitutional rights and drastically reinterpret existing laws. Today, the fundamental right of a woman to reproductive freedom rests on the votes of six members of the Supreme Court — five of whom are over 75. That right could easily disappear during a second Reagan term.	The unborn child has a fundamental individual right to life which cannot be infringed. We therefore reaffirm our support for a human life amendment to the Constitution, and we endorse legislation to make clear that the Fourteenth Amendment's protections apply to unborn children. We oppose the use of public revenues for abortion and will eliminate funding for organizations which advocate or support abortion. We commend the efforts of those individuals and religious and private organizations that are providing positive alternatives to abortion by meeting the physical, emotional, and financial needs of pregnant women and offering adoption services where needed.
	We applaud President Reagan's fine record of judicial appointments, and we reaffirm our support for the appointment of judges at all levels of the judiciary who respect traditional family values and the sanctity of innocent human life.
1988	
We further believe that we must work for the adoption of the Equal Rights Amendment to the	That the unborn child has a fundamental individual right to life which cannot be infringed. We

Democrat	Republican
Constitution; that the fundamental right of reproductive choice should be guaranteed regardless of ability to pay.	therefore reaffirm our support for a human life amendment to the Constitution, and we endorse legislation to make clear that the Fourteenth Amendment's protections apply to unborn children. We oppose the use of public revenues for abortion and will eliminate funding for organizations which advocate or support abortion. We commend the efforts of those individuals and religious and private organizations that are providing positive alternatives to abortion by meeting the physical, emotional, and financial needs of pregnant women and offering adoption services where needed.

We applaud President Reagan's fine record of judicial appointments, and we reaffirm our support for the appointment of judges at all levels of the judiciary who respect traditional family values and the sanctity of innocent human life. |
| **1992**

Democrats stand behind the right of every woman to choose, consistent with *Roe* v. *Wade*, regardless of ability to pay, and support a national law to protect that right.

It is a fundamental constitutional liberty that individual | We believe the unborn child has a fundamental individual right to life which cannot be infringed. We therefore reaffirm our support for a human life amendment to the Constitution, and we endorse legislation to make clear that the Fourteenth |

Democrat	Republican
Americans — not government — can best take responsibility for making the most difficult and intensely personal decisions regarding reproduction. The goal of our nation must be to make abortion less necessary, not more difficult or more dangerous. We pledge to support contraceptive research, family planning, comprehensive family life education, and policies that support healthy childbearing and enable parents to care most effectively for their children.	Amendment's protections apply to unborn children. We oppose using public revenues for abortion and will not fund organizations which advocate it. We commend those who provide alternatives to abortion by meeting the needs of mothers and offering adoption services. We reaffirm our support for appointment of judges who respect traditional family values and the sanctity of innocent human life.
1996	
The Democratic Party stands behind the right of every woman to choose, consistent with *Roe* v. *Wade*, and regardless of ability to pay. President Clinton took executive action to make sure that the right to make such decisions is protected for all Americans. Over the last four years, we have taken action to end the gag rule and ensure safety at family planning and women's health clinics. We believe it is a fundamental constitutional liberty that individual Americans — not government — can best take responsibility for making the most difficult and intensely personal decisions regarding reproduction.	The unborn child has a fundamental individual right to life which cannot be infringed. We support a human life amendment to the Constitution and we endorse legislation to make clear that the Fourteenth Amendment's protections apply to unborn children. Our purpose is to have legislative and judicial protection of that right against those who perform abortions. We oppose using public revenues for abortion and will not fund organizations which advocate it. We support the appointment of judges who respect traditional family values and the sanctity of innocent human life.

Democrat	Republican
The Democratic Party is a party of inclusion. We respect the individual conscience of each American on this difficult issue, and we welcome all our members to participate at every level of our party. Our goal is to make abortion less necessary and more rare, not more difficult and more dangerous. We support contraceptive research, family planning, comprehensive family life education, and policies that support healthy childbearing. For four years in a row, we have increased support for family planning. The abortion rate is dropping. Now we must continue to support efforts to reduce unintended pregnancies, and we call on all Americans to take personal responsibility to meet this important goal.	Our goal is to ensure that women with problem pregnancies have the kind of support, material and otherwise, they need for themselves and for their babies, not to be punitive towards those for whose difficult situation we have only compassion. We oppose abortion, but our pro-life agenda does not include punitive action against women who have an abortion. We salute those who provide alternatives to abortion and offer adoption services. Republicans in Congress took the lead in expanding assistance both for the costs of adoption and for the continuing care of adoptive children with special needs. Bill Clinton vetoed our adoption tax credit the first time around — and opposed our efforts to remove racial barriers to adoption — before joining in this long overdue measure of support for adoptive families. Worse than that, he vetoed the ban on partial-birth abortions, a procedure denounced by a committee of the American Medical Association and rightly branded as four-fifths infanticide. We applaud Bob Dole's commitment to revoke the Clinton executive orders concerning abortion and to sign into law an end to partial-birth abortions.

Democrat	Republican
2000	
The Democratic Party stands behind the right of every woman to choose, consistent with *Roe* v. *Wade*, and regardless of ability to pay. We believe it is a fundamental constitutional liberty that individual Americans—not government—can best take responsibility for making the most difficult and intensely personal decisions regarding reproduction. This year's Supreme Court rulings show to us all that eliminating a woman's right to choose is only one justice away. That's why the stakes in this election are as high as ever.	The Supreme Court's recent decision, prohibiting states from banning partial-birth abortions — a procedure denounced by a committee of the American Medical Association and rightly branded as four-fifths infanticide — shocks the conscience of the nation. As a country, we must keep our pledge to the first guarantee of the Declaration of Independence. That is why we say the unborn child has a fundamental individual right to life which cannot be infringed. We support a human life amendment to the Constitution and we endorse legislation to make clear that the Fourteenth Amendment's protections apply to unborn children.
Our goal is to make abortion less necessary and more rare, not more difficult and more dangerous. We support contraceptive research, family planning, comprehensive family life education, and policies that support healthy childbearing. The abortion rate is dropping. Now we must continue to support efforts to reduce unintended pregnancies, and we call on all Americans to take personal responsibility to meet this important goal.	Our purpose is to have legislative and judicial protection of that right against those who perform abortions. We oppose using public revenues for abortion and will not fund organizations which advocate it. We support the appointment of judges who respect traditional family values and the sanctity of innocent human life.
The Democratic Party is a party of inclusion. We respect the individual conscience of each American on this difficult issue,	Our goal is to ensure that women with problem pregnancies have the kind of support, material and otherwise, they need for themselves

Democrat	Republican
and we welcome all our members to participate at every level of our party. This is why we are proud to put into our platform the very words which Republicans refused to let Bob Dole put into their 1996 platform and which they refused to even consider putting in their platform in 2000: "While the party remains steadfast in its commitment to advancing its historic principles and ideals, we also recognize that members of our party have deeply held and sometimes differing views on issues of personal conscience like abortion and capital punishment. We view this diversity of views as a source of strength, not as a sign of weakness, and we welcome into our ranks all Americans who may hold differing positions on these and other issues. Recognizing that tolerance is a virtue, we are committed to resolving our differences in a spirit of civility, hope and mutual respect."	and for their babies, not to be punitive towards those for whose difficult situation we have only compassion. We oppose abortion, but our pro-life agenda does not include punitive action against women who have an abortion. We salute those who provide alternatives to abortion and offer adoption services, and we commend congressional Republicans for expanding assistance to adopting families and for removing racial barriers to adoption. The impact of those measures and of our Adoption and Safe Families Act of 1997 has been spectacular. Adoptions out of foster care have jumped forty percent and the incidence of child abuse and neglect has actually declined. We second Governor Bush's call to make permanent the adoption tax credit and expand it to $7,500.
2004 Because we believe in the privacy and equality of women, we stand proudly for a woman's right to choose, consistent with *Roe* v. *Wade*, and regardless of her ability to pay. We stand firmly against Republican	As a country, we must keep our pledge to the first guarantee of the Declaration of Independence. That is why we say the unborn child has a fundamental individual right to life which cannot be infringed. We

Democrat	Republican
efforts to undermine that right. At the same time, we strongly support family planning and adoption incentives. Abortion should be safe, legal, and rare.	support a human life amendment to the Constitution and we endorse legislation to make it clear that the Fourteenth Amendment's protections apply to unborn children. Our purpose is to have legislative and judicial protection of that right against those who perform abortions. We oppose using public revenues for abortion and will not fund organizations which advocate it. We support the appointment of judges who respect traditional family values and the sanctity of innocent human life.
	Our goal is to ensure that women with problem pregnancies have the kind of support, material and otherwise, they need for themselves and for their babies, not to be punitive towards those for whose difficult situation we have only compassion. We oppose abortion, but our pro-life agenda does not include punitive action against women who have an abortion. We salute those who provide alternatives to abortion and offer adoption services, and we commend congressional Republicans for expanding assistance to adopting families and for removing racial barriers to adoption. We join the president in supporting crisis

Democrat	Republican
	pregnancy programs and parental notification laws. And we applaud President Bush for allowing states to extend health care coverage to unborn children.

We praise the president for his bold leadership in defense of life. We praise him for signing the Born Alive Infants Protection Act. This important legislation ensures that every infant born alive — including an infant who survives an abortion procedure — is considered a person under federal law.

We praise Republicans in Congress for passing, with strong bipartisan support, a ban on the inhumane procedure known as partial birth abortion. And we applaud President Bush for signing legislation outlawing partial birth abortion and for vigorously defending it in the courts.

In signing the partial birth abortion ban, President Bush reminded us that "the most basic duty of government is to defend the life of the innocent. Every person, however frail or vulnerable, has a place and a purpose in this world." We affirm the inherent dignity and worth of all people. We oppose the non-consensual withholding of care |

Democrat	Republican
	or treatment because of disability, age, or infirmity, just as we oppose euthanasia and assisted suicide, which especially endanger the poor and those on the margins of society. We support President Bush's decision to restore the Drug Enforcement Administration's policy that controlled substances shall not be used for assisted suicide. We applaud congressional Republicans for their leadership against those abuses and their pioneering legislation to focus research and treatment resources on the alleviation of pain and the care of terminally ill patients.

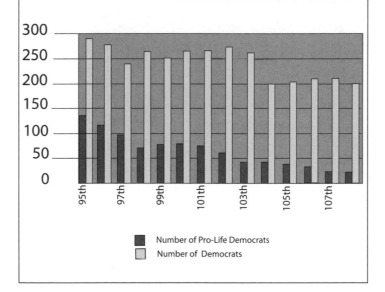

Attachment 2
Democrats Are Losing Power Over the Pro-life Issue

In the 95th Congress, we held a 292-seat majority, with 42% of Democrats being pro-life. Republicans are taking seats in pro-life districts we could win. We now hold 204 seats with 14.7% pro-life Democrats.

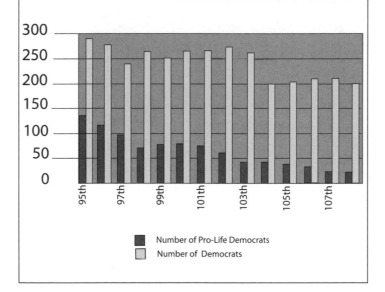

- ■ Number of Pro-Life Democrats
- ▫ Number of Democrats

Attachment 3
The 95-10 Initiative

A comprehensive plan that will reduce the number of abortions by 95 percent in the next 10 years by promoting abstinence, personal responsibility, adoptions, and support for women and families who are facing unplanned pregnancy.

The 95-10 Initiative seeks to reduce the number of abortions in America through federal, state, and local efforts as well as support and encouragement to volunteers and dedicated people on the front lines helping pregnant women. Much attention has been given to ending abortion or keeping it legal. We believe that we must do more to reduce the abortion rate by helping and supporting pregnant women.

Preventing pregnancy is an important part of reducing the abortion rate in America. There are several ways to address prevention, but there is no clear consensus because of ethical, religious, or personal reasons. There are several bills before Congress that address pregnancy prevention. While we have not endorsed a particular bill, we support finding the most effective way to reduce unplanned pregnancies. We cannot deny that abstinence is the only sure way to prevent pregnancy, but we also cannot turn our heads and pretend that our children are not engaging in risky behavior or the fact that contraception is not 100 percent effective. The federal government has made a commitment to support prevention efforts and allocated a record $288.3 million in FY 2005 for family planning under title X. The program provides access to contraceptive supplies and information to all who want and need them. A priority is given to low-income persons.

The federal government has not made that same commitment to those who wish to carry their children to term. We support **helping pregnant women,** many who believe abortion is their only option. Congressman Lincoln Davis (D-TN) and pro-life Democrats in Congress who share this same commitment will introduce the Pregnant Women Support Act, a comprehensive bill to provide support for pregnant women who want to carry their child to term. Some of the programs included are: establishing a toll-free number to direct women to places that will provide support and pregnancy counseling and childcare on university campuses, requiring doctors to provide accurate information to patients receiving positive results from prenatal testing and counseling in maternity group homes, making the Adoption Tax Credits permanent, and increasing tax credits. The legislation would eliminate pregnancy as a pre-existing condition, supports informed consent for abortion services, increases funding for domestic violence programs, and requires the SCHIP to cover pregnant women and unborn children. It further provides free home visits by registered nurses for new mothers, incentives to reduce teen pregnancy,